RODALE'S HOME DESIGN SERIES™

KITCHENS

by the Editors of
Rodale's New Shelter® magazine

 Rodale Press, Emmaus, Pennsylvania

Printed in the United States of America on recycled
paper containing a high percentage of de-inked fiber.

Senior Editor: Ray Wolf
Series Editor: Margaret Lydic Balitas
Writers: Craig Canine, Jeremiah Eck, Sidney J. Hymes,
     Michael Lafavore, Catherine M. Poole,
     Marguerite Smolen, Michael Stoner, and
     Beverly Wilson
Technical Reviewer: Fred Matlack
Editorial Assistance: Kerri Balliet and Bobbie Wanamaker
Copy Editor: Dolores Plikaitis

Director of Photography: T. L. Gettings
Series Photography Editor: Mitchell T. Mandel
Styling of Front Cover Photo (hardcover): Renee R. Keith
Styling of Front Cover Photo (paperback): J. C. Vera

Art Director: Jerry O Brien
Series Art Director and Book Designer: Karen A. Schell
Project Assistant: Denise Mirabello
Illustrator: John Carlance

Library of Congress Cataloging in Publication Data
Main entry under title:

Kitchens.

     (Rodale's home design series)
     Includes index.
     1. Kitchens. I. Rodale's new shelter. II Series.
NA8330.K59   1986   747.7'97   85-28269
ISBN   0-87857-605-3   hardcover
ISBN   0-87857-606-1   paperback

2 4 6 8 10 9 7 5 3 1   hardcover
2 4 6 8 10 9 7 5 3 1   paperback

CONTENTS

2282248

ACKNOWLEDGMENTS

A host of people worked together to make this book the success that it is. The original idea for a book on kitchen design belongs to Ray Wolf, senior editor, who was the overseer for this project. He, along with editor Margaret Lydic Balitas, gave shape to the book, and they are responsible for the information contained herein. Writers Craig Canine, Jeremiah Eck, Sidney J. Hymes, Michael Lafavore, Catherine M. Poole, Marguerite Smolen, Michael Stoner, and Beverly Wilson gave substance to the book's outline and used their expertise to write intelligently about kitchen design. Technical reviewer Fred Matlack ensured that our information was correct, and copy editor Dolores Plikaitis made certain that we made good use of the English language. Kerri Balliet and Bobbie Wanamaker added their special research skills to the book project.

The Rodale Press Photography Department, under the direction of T. L. Gettings, is responsible for the bulk of the beautiful photographs. Special thanks to the photographers who shot most of the photos: series photography editor Mitchell T. Mandel, and J. Michael Kanouff. Thanks, too, to photographers Angelo Caggiano, Adam B. Laipson, and Mark Lenny; photo stylists Kathy Boucher, Renee R. Keith, and J. C. Vera; and photo librarian Rose Reichl. Several manufacturers lent photographs to us for use in this book, and we thank them.

Executive designer Karen A. Schell lent her considerable book design skills to create a work of art. Denise Mirabello, project assistant, very ably assisted her. John Carlance's illustrations clearly show how well-designed kitchens work.

Many thanks to everyone who helped to locate stunning kitchens throughout the United States, including Cathy Barnett-Charles, J. Michael Kanouff, James Kershaw, Robert Lidsky, Larry McClung, Mitchell T. Mandel, Roger Moyer, Sharon Oliger, Craig Shutt, and Susan Smith, as well as the writers of this book.

We especially thank the 22 homeowners who graciously welcomed us into their kitchens and made "Gallery: A Tour of Fine Kitchens" possible. Many thanks, too, to others who invited our photographers into their homes and willingly spoke to us about their kitchens. We are indebted to the numerous architects and designers mentioned in this book, who shared their designs and secrets for successful kitchens with us.

DESIGN IDEAS
NEW AND REMODELED KITCHENS

A New Version of the Hearth

In the back of your mind, do you have a vague sense that something is not right with most modern houses? They are often not really homes at all but commodities passed around on the real estate market. They are loaded with features that are supposed to improve their resale value but don't make the houses more livable.

Many designers and architects believe that there is a strong relationship between the quality of space in a home and the happiness of the family inside. The contention is simple: A home and its hearth are synonymous. Most houses are *not* homes but could be with the addition of a hearth. A "hearth" is not just a fireplace but a room—with or without a fireplace—that naturally draws a family to it for warmth and activity.

At one time in the history of this country, the hearth was, literally, the center of the house and the hub of family activity. The early English settlers on the Atlantic seaboard constructed simple houses having rooms with names such as parlor, hall, or keeping room. The parlor was used for formal occasions, while the hall and keeping room were used for work and family recreation. The element tying these spaces together was the central chimney, a huge structural and heat-producing mass, equipped with built-in ovens, swinging cranes, and assorted hanging pots. All family activities centered around it. As Americans became more affluent and life more sophisticated, house plans became more complex, yet they retained an essential centrality and focus in the hearth room. And for a long time the family truly functioned as a unit.

In the South where the climate was less severe, the typical early house had two chimneys, one at either end. The central element was the great hall. Rising two stories and usually containing a grand staircase, it allowed air to circulate freely from large windows on either side. Thus, like the northern hearth, it supplied what was environmentally essential and served as a unifying element in the plan. It was the hub of family activity.

For a brief period of time in the late nineteenth century, these two house types from North and South merged into what historians now call the Shingle style, generally loved by all for its sense of individuality and coziness. In this style, the two forms

merged into a combination of the great hall and the central fireplace. The living hall, as this new room came to be called, had a fireplace, stair, benches inside and out, and usually was at least two stories high. It was an arbitrator of family activity, connecting the private life of the upstairs with the social life of the downstairs.

Unfortunately, with only rare exceptions, we have not produced homes of this quality for a hundred years. Coincidentally, over these hundred years we have also witnessed the gradual loosening of family ties and the disintegration of the family. Should we blame the social order *or* should we blame the house?

The typical modern suburban house is utterly devoid of spirit and lacks any sense of focus. "Living" rooms, "family" rooms, dens, and dining rooms all conspire to destroy opportunities for family togetherness. The food preparation and dining rooms are often completely separated—as in the time when cooks and maids were common. So-called living rooms often receive more attention in planning and decorating than other rooms but then are rarely used. Dens and "rec" rooms are sometimes added to provide a place for family activities, but frequently they become the children's exclusive terrain and exaggerate rather than alleviate the schism between parents and children. In most cases one parent, usually the mother, must isolate herself in the kitchen at mealtimes and then is excluded from activities happening elsewhere in the house.

This book is about kitchen design, but it is about more. It is about how to turn your kitchen into a hearth room, how to make your kitchen the center for family activities, how to breathe vitality into this most important living space. If we can reestablish the kitchen with a genuine family focus, we will be lighting the hearth fire once again.

We can call this room by many names—a living hall, a hearth room, a kitchen/living room, a great-room kitchen, or a combination room. Despite the name given to this room, you will easily recognize its use. It combines the functions of the kitchen, dining room, den, family room, and office. This great room can resemble the northern hearth because it forms a true center of family activity and very often contains a fireplace or woodstove. Or, it can resemble the southern version with the double height spaces and liberal use of glass, which fill the room with sunshine and create cross ventilation in the summer. You have three options in creating a hearth room in your home. You can build a new house, find an existing house and renovate it, or change what you already have.

If you're building a new house, consider combining functions of rooms. Ask yourself: Can the kitchen and family room be one room? Do you really need large bedrooms, considering the amount of time you spend there? Avoid thinking of living areas as "rooms." Rather, approach them as formal/informal, public/private areas.

When looking for an existing house, take a hard look at the layout to see if it fits your needs or has the *potential* to fit those needs. Imagine a wall removed or a ceiling opened up. Don't overlook a structurally sound, small house. You can use the money you saved buying the smaller house to renovate it to suit you.

If you already have a house and feel it doesn't fulfill your needs, your options are *not* limited. Each house has its own unique solution. Locate the true hearth of your home—the place where you feel most comfortable and most often find your family and friends gathered. There's a good chance that it is the existing kitchen. Consciously turn this space into the headquarters for family activities. Move all the kitchen appliances into the new hearth room together with your books, dining room, sofa, easy chair, or hobby equipment. Don't be afraid

The "hearth" in this great-room kitchen is the sunspace, which washes the room with light.

to move a few walls or add windows to let in sunlight.

No family should consider a new kitchen or the renovation of an existing kitchen without taking into account the need for this new hearth. The new hearths will in many ways be a synthesis of their antecedents in the northern and southern houses. The challenge is before you to create a focal point in your home so that once again the hearth fire burns strong and sure.

What Else Is New?

Now that kitchens are multi-purpose rooms, we demand designs that are both functional and good-looking. We want a subtle integration of cabinets, appliances, and furnishings, so that everything looks "at home" in our kitchens. Curves and soft lines, both popular now, contribute to making us feel at ease in our kitchens no matter what we do there—cook, entertain, visit with friends, watch TV.

One strong trend these days is to select European-style laminate cabinets. A recent nationwide survey of 2,000 kitchen-cabinet dealers revealed that 20 percent of their sales were European-style laminate kitchens. That does not mean that high-tech laminates are replacing wood. Finely crafted wood cabinets are still in demand. And wood is an elegant, yet warm, accent on laminate cabinets and counter edges. Ceilings and floors of wood are also popular.

Perhaps the primary consideration in kitchen design is color. The new laminates offer virtually any color you can imagine for your new kitchen, but the most popular colors in *both* wood and laminate kitchens are neutral tones. Whites and grays and light wood are the colors of choice.

Another major trend in kitchens is a demand for high-performance, energy-efficient appliances. And again the colors of choice are either neutrals or the dramatic look of black glass fronts. We want these appliances to look built in, which is possible now that appliances are manufactured to fit under upper cabinets, to be easily concealed by trim kits, or to fit the exact depth of a standard base counter. In

Kitchens now feature high-performance, energy-efficient appliances. Black-glass fronts give a dramatic look to wood or laminate cabinets.

fact, in some kitchens the appliances are so well integrated that it is difficult to "see" them at first glance. The trend in European-style cabinets calls for European-style appliances. Appliances, both big and small and both European and American, do their work without attracting attention, or, if they do attract our attention, they are so well-designed that they are nearly works of art.

We are also now using building products in our kitchens that for a long time were used in other parts of the home. Wood floors are moving into the kitchen—replacing, in many cases, vinyl and carpeting. Special finishes repel moisture and can hold up against the wear and tear of kitchen traffic. Tile, always a favorite in baths, has boldly moved onto kitchen floors, backsplashes, walls, and countertops. Skylights, clerestory

Twenty percent of all new kitchens today have European-style cabinetry.

windows, raised ceilings, and state-of-the-art lighting systems are now as much at home in the kitchen as any place else in the house. And since the kitchen is such an important living space, fine furniture and accessories are an important part of many kitchen decors.

Finally, we look at our homes as a major investment—sometimes our biggest investment. We want to invest the thousands of dollars we will spend in our kitchens wisely. We want designs that we can enjoy and easily live with day in and day out *and* ones that increase the resale value of our homes.

We expect a lot from our kitchens—elegance in design, high performance from appliances, and a sound investment. This is all possible no matter what the style—country, high tech, city chic, or European.

The Too Small Kitchen

An ambitious cook may find the small kitchens common in city apartments and houses from the 1940s frustrating, but sometimes it is simply not possible to steal additional space from a surrounding room to enlarge a kitchen. If you face this problem, you can still make your kitchen work better in the space it occupies. With a few changes you can make a too small kitchen into one that is just right.

As a first step, try to open it up by enlarging or adding a window, installing a skylight, or breaking through an interior wall into another room. You may not gain actual space in the kitchen, but the effect will make the room seem larger. So will white or light-colored walls, floors, and cabinets.

In a small kitchen, organization is paramount. Every inch of space must have one function, preferably three. When the sink is not in use, it might be covered with a tray of condiments that can be moved to the table when you're washing dishes. Or a cutting board may be set over the sink for chopping or dicing vegetables. An island can be used as a food preparation surface, then cleaned off and used for dining.

Examine the storage possibilities offered by every square inch of space. You can gain

Once too small and dingy, this kitchen is now just right because of a few major additions: the large bay window and window seat, an island with drop leaves, and the three-tier table. Light-colored walls, floors, and ceilings and track lighting make this kitchen seem larger than it is. New cabinets provide efficient storage.

overhead storage by eliminating the soffits above the cabinets and installing the cabinets to the ceiling. Hang pots and utensils on the wall underneath overhead cabinets. Full-length pantry closets used in place of base and wall cabinets can provide a section of floor-to-ceiling enclosed storage. Gain counter space by adding foldaway shelves to the ends or sides of counters.

In selecting cookware and utensils for a small kitchen, follow the same principles that you use in organizing your kitchen. If something can't serve more than one function, decide if you really need it. You may also want to alter your cooking style and the way you shop for food. You can reduce the size of your pantry and refrigerator if you learn to keep only staples on hand, shopping for other foods only when needed.

This table's three tiers pivot to allow it to take many shapes, which greatly increases the surface area for dining, food preparation, or anything else.

7

QUESTIONS TO ANSWER BEFORE YOU BEGIN

In the classes that Beverly Wilson, a kitchen-design professional at the Owner Builder Center (OBC) in Berkeley, California, teaches, many students tell her that the questions she asks are the most valuable part of the course. Now we're giving Beverly a chance to ask *you* these questions.

There are no correct answers, and it may not seem like you're learning much as you answer them, but you are. If you don't take enough time to thoroughly plan out that "new look," you may end up out of money before you finish, or with a kitchen that somehow falls short of your dream. Don't let that happen to you.

Are You Remodeling or Starting from Scratch?

The information in this book will help both those who are remodeling and those who are starting from scratch by designing a kitchen as part of a new home. Remember, newness doesn't ensure good design.

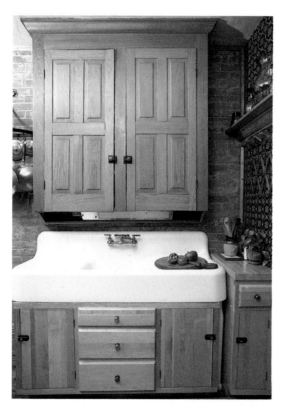

Can you save something from your old kitchen? The upper cabinet is original to the house, built nearly a century ago. The new base cabinet, built to match the upper one, fits smartly beneath the old sink.

If you're remodeling, ask yourself why. Then make a list of your reasons for making the change. Perhaps your kitchen is out-of-date. The layout is impossible. There aren't enough storage areas, or there's too little counter space. Your home's traffic patterns run right through the middle of the kitchen. The windows are too small or too big or too high, or they look out onto a blank wall.

Ask yourself how extensive you want the remodeling to be. Remodeling can be just sprucing up your old kitchen, for example, by replacing worn flooring. Or it can involve extensive rearranging or remodeling. It can mean enlarging the present kitchen or moving to a new room. It can even mean building on a new room.

How Old Is Your House and What Is Its Style?

Do you want to work with that style, or will you do something entirely different? You may decide to give your San Francisco Victorian or your Vermont farmhouse a sleek, high-tech kitchen that completely ignores the architectural details of the rest of the house. A totally different style can work, although most remodelers tend to stay a little closer to the styles of the surrounding rooms. If you want your new kitchen to fit right in, try to salvage door and window moldings that may get torn out during your project. New matching moldings may be hard to find and are very expensive to make.

Look closely at your old kitchen. There may be parts you can and want to keep. The more you can save of the existing kitchen, the less expensive the new one will be. For instance, it's costly to move plumbing, so most people try to work around the sink. By the same token, changing the location of the range or switching from gas to electric will add substantially to your costs.

What Do You Want in Your New Kitchen?

If you are remodeling *or* starting from scratch, make a list of what you want in your new kitchen. Include everything—big necessities, more counter space, little luxuries, a place to display your cactus garden. Don't worry yet about the relative importance of each item; just get them all down.

Who Will Use the Kitchen and How Will It Be Used?

If one of your cooks is very tall, you may want to raise your counters above the 36-inch standard. And built-in steps that slide out of the way can make the kitchen more accessible to children. A left-handed person may have trouble working in a kitchen designed for a right-handed cook. If a handicapped person will be using the kitchen, you'll have to make special provisions. Older cooks also need to be taken into consideration, with storage areas that can be reached without too much bending or stretching.

On the other hand, if you are remodeling with resale in mind, you'll want to design a space that appeals to a large audience. Even if you don't want a dishwasher, leave space and install plumbing for one beside the sink. A 24-inch cabinet can fill that spot in the meantime. Stick to standard counter heights, too, and leave out the built-in wok. Build a neutral kitchen so new owners can add their personal touches.

You must consider how your family cooks, how often, and for how many people. If two people are going to be working in the kitchen most of the time, you'll need two work areas so the cooks won't keep bumping into each other. If budget and space allow, two sinks are nice to have in a two-cook kitchen.

How will you use your kitchen? This island is for informal dining and food preparation and also serves as a gathering center for parties.

How you entertain is an important element in kitchen design. If you specialize in potluck suppers, you won't have to add much to your kitchen to accommodate even large groups. But if you like to host cocktail parties and serve all kinds of little tidbits, you may want to invest in two ovens so that you can bake many trays of food at one time. If your forte is formal entertaining and dining, you'll probably need extra storage space for dishes and linens.

If cooking is your hobby, plan a place to keep all of your favorite cookbooks, and design special cupboards to hold the specialty items you've collected. Leave extra room, since your collection will undoubtedly keep growing.

What Kinds of Gadgets Will You Need in Your New Kitchen?

Make a list of all of the equipment you have now. Next to each item mark whether you use it often, seldom, or never—or if you think you may use it in the future. This list

9

will help you plan storage needs for the kitchen. It may even prompt you to toss out a few things.

What Are Your Cleanup Habits?

Don't expect them to change, just because you're getting a new kitchen. If you let dirty dishes accumulate until the end of the meal, you'll need to leave ample space near the sink for stacking them. Some people do manage to wash and put away everything as they go along, even when they're preparing a huge meal. If you're one of those, you can afford to skimp on that section of counter.

Will the Kitchen Be More Than Just a Place to Cook or Will It Be a Private Kitchen?

Now that the great-room kitchen is once again the center of family living, the whole family is liable to take a hand in the cooking. With that in mind—and given the space you have to work with—what activities are you going to be planning for? Will this be a sewing room, playroom, study hall, laundry, dining room, family office?

Some people prefer to be alone in the kitchen, out of the flow of activities. They don't want guests perched around watching them whip up the last of dinner. If you feel that way, plan your kitchen so you can have your privacy.

What Kind of Storage Do You Want and Need?

Consider your shopping routine. If you go to the store once a month and buy in bulk, you'll need a lot of storage space. It doesn't have to be in the kitchen, though. You could set aside an area in your garage or cellar and use it like a very convenient store; in the kitchen itself, you can keep only what you'll be using in the next few days. If you often cook from scratch, you'll want a space to store flours and spices, in a spot within reach of where you'll use them.

Above and beyond its architectural style, you must think about how you want your new kitchen to look. It can range from very tidy, with everything behind closed doors, to organized clutter, with everything out in

Will you dine in your kitchen? This table conveniently rolls out and then slides away for storage.

the open. Most of us will compromise somewhere in between these two extremes. Open storage may bring back memories of grandmother's pantry with shelves all around, but don't use open storage below your counters—it's too difficult to keep dust out down there.

To plan your storage areas, make another list or chart. Decide whether you want open or closed storage or a combination for your foodstuffs, small appliances, cooking equipment, pots and pans, dishes, spices, cookbooks, and everything else.

What about Money?

Do you have enough to do the whole job at one time? If not, you can still do all of your planning now and then break the work schedule into segments to match the available funds. Are you planning to keep any of your old appliances, cupboards, or windows? Would you like to replace them later on? How much of the construction costs can be offset by labor from your friends and family?

In remodeling, labor costs are big money.

Can You Help with the Design and Construction of Your New Kitchen?

Consider how much of the design and construction work on your new kitchen you can do and are willing to do. Do your homework and then honestly assess your abilities. When necessary, hire the right professionals.

Are you getting impatient with all of these questions? You are probably anxious to start ripping out walls if you are remodeling, or you are champing at the bit to get your new kitchen installed in your new house. Thorough planning is important.

Do you expect your kitchen to be more than just a place to prepare food? This office center contains cookbooks, a TV, a message center, and a collection of duck decoys.

How will your new kitchen look? European-style cabinetry with a combination of open and closed storage sets the style here.

Sizing Up Your Present Kitchen

Imagine your house sliced in two horizontally a few feet above the floor. If you could pluck off the top half, you could look straight down on your kitchen. You'd see the floor, the major appliances, the countertops, the edges of your doors and windows. You'd also be able to see inside your walls where you'd find wiring, plumbing, ductwork, insulation. You'd be getting a real education—an invaluable one, now that you're ready to remodel.

In this section you'll learn how to measure and draw up the plan of your existing kitchen and the areas that surround it. The drawing you end up with should look a lot like the imaginary bird's-eye view described above. Putting your old kitchen down on paper this way will give you a better feel for the space you have to work with.

For some of you, this step may not be necessary. Many kitchens work fine the way they are; they just look old. In that kind of kitchen, simply changing the cabinets and replacing the appliances may satisfy your need for something different. If that's all you're doing, there's no reason to draw up a complete plan.

For the rest of you, who have bigger things in mind, plan to spend at least a couple of hours drawing a plan. You won't need special training, but it's nice to have a helper who can hold the end of your measuring tape, check numbers, and record the information. Your first drawing can be rough; you're just trying to get down all the facts. Later, you can go back and draw up a finished plan.

Going to Work

Your first step will be to gather together all of the tools you're going to need. Here are the ones you'll need:

Retractable steel measuring tape. A heavy-duty, 25-foot tape is handy, although you can get by with a smaller one. Don't use a yardstick or a cloth sewing tape measure; those aren't meant for this kind of work.

Graph paper. Get the kind with ¼-inch squares. Graph paper with five squares to the inch looks very similar, but that size will cause confusion in your drawing.

Architectural scale. This tool is not absolutely necessary but will make the job a lot easier and more fun. (See "How to Use an Architectural Scale" on page 128.)

Ruler or straightedge. You'll need it for drawing straight lines.

T-square. Although not a necessity, a T-square is useful if you happen to have one around.

Tracing paper. When you're trying out different ideas, tracing paper will come in handy.

Blueprint paper. This is a luxury if you don't have easy access to a blueprint store. The large size is very helpful and much easier than taping smaller pages together. And it will let you make copies of the final drawing.

Once you've assembled your tool kit, you'll be ready to start drawing. Tape a piece of graph paper to a smooth board. This will give you something sturdy to write and draw on. Then, starting in one corner of the room,

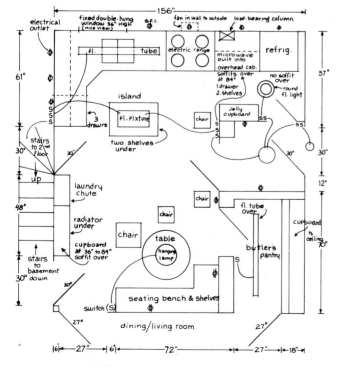

Carefully make a sketch of your existing kitchen so you can see its potential for remodeling.

measure your first wall, record its length, and draw a line to scale on the graph paper. A scale of ½ inch to the foot is a reasonable one to work with, which means that a 6-foot wall will be a 3-inch line on your drawing. Mark down the actual measured length of the wall, in inches, next to the line you've drawn. (Kitchen measurements are always recorded in inches. Since 158 inches does not immediately bring a size to mind, note feet and inches underneath.) Be sure to measure as accurately as possible. A quarter-inch lost or gained here and there can add up—to trouble.

Next, go back and measure the parts of your first wall. On your drawing, note the distance from the corner to the first thing that gets in your way—probably the edge of the molding around a window or door. Then measure the door or window, including molding, and then the next section of wall. When you've reached the next corner, the sum of all of the parts should equal the total length of the wall. Now measure the movable part of each window and the width of each door. Note the molding widths, too.

Continue around the room measuring and drawing all of the walls and parts of walls. If you've measured accurately, you should end up where you started. If you don't, try redrawing the space using the measurements you have taken. If you are still off, remeasure. This can be very frustrating, but resist the impulse to cheat. Eventually, you'll have to reckon with any discrepancies between your drawing and what's really there.

If you're not going to be expanding your kitchen, the thickness of the walls is not important: Leave them as single pencil lines. But if you are expanding, add thickness to the walls. Walls are usually 4½ to 5 inches thick; check yours at a door or window, being careful not to include the thicknesses of the moldings.

With the walls, doors, and windows taken care of, draw in everything else that's taking up space in your kitchen. Note any chimneys or flues, and mention whether these are still being used. Add the cabinets, and write in what's below the countertop: a cabinet drawer that opens this way or that, the number of drawers, special features like a bread box or an old icebox.

On your plan, draw an arc for each door swing, and note the heights of windows and how they open. Locate and draw in all outlets and switches. Draw a curved line from each switch to whatever it operates. Add the major appliances, and record whether the stove is gas or electric.

Mark down the height—or heights—of your ceiling. When you plan your new kitchen, you'll have to decide how tall the upper cabinets will be. Seven feet is the standard height for the top edge, but that's not sacrosanct. You may decide to extend your cabinets all the way to the ceiling. Or you may choose to make soffits—closed-off spaces above the cabinets. Or you can leave that area open, for displaying your collectibles.

Locate any pipes or furnace ducts in the walls of your kitchen, and draw these into your plan. If there is a bathroom above the kitchen, determine where the plumbing lines for it pass through your walls. If you are planning to remove walls or change doors and windows, pipes and ductwork can be difficult and expensive to move.

Label all of the rooms surrounding the kitchen. If you're planning to expand, you may find it helpful to do a quick sketch of your entire home's floor plan and the layout of your grounds. This doesn't have to be as accurate as your kitchen drawing, but it will help to remind you of traffic flow and the rooms affected by the kitchen. Note the view from your kitchen windows, and be sure to locate north on your drawing. If you're planning a skylight, make sure it is positioned so that it won't let in late afternoon summer sun—that can broil you in short order.

After you've finished a roughly drawn plan, redo it on fresh paper. This is when it is nice to have large blueprint paper. Decide which side of the drawing will be the top and then do all of your writing in the same direction. Otherwise, you'll have to keep turning the page as you go around the room. Use a sharp pencil to print, as neatly as possible, the information you've gathered. If there's no room on the plan to put the information exactly where it should go, write it elsewhere on the page, and draw an arrow

If you can't expand the size of your kitchen, it's still possible to open it up to other living areas. Knock out a load-bearing wall, but leave a "pillar" for support.

to the appropriate spot. The arrow's shaft should curve, so that you won't confuse it with a wall or other construction detail.

A carefully rendered drawing is invaluable in helping you to see what new arrangement will best fit the space you have—or the space you can create by moving a few walls, doors, or windows.

Major Changes

If you are going to be removing a wall, first make sure it isn't holding up the roof. Load-bearing walls usually run perpendicular to the ceiling joists. These walls can be removed, but only after you've found some other way to support the joists. If you have any doubts about how to do that, get detailed advice from someone who does know how, or call in a professional.

Moving a door can work wonders on your traffic flow and make an impossible

kitchen workable. It can also add considerably to the cost of your project, but it just might be the best place to splurge. Look at your plan, and consider all of the implications of this change. Any outlets or switches where you plan to put a new door will have to be moved. Ditto for pipes and furnace ducts. The adjoining rooms will also be involved. The wall on the other side of your new door will have to be repaired, repainted, and may need to be outfitted with new moldings.

Replacing a small window with a larger one can be quite easy, although you'll still have to look out for problems with wiring, plumbing, and ductwork. Going in the other direction, though, can be more difficult. If you exchange a big window for a smaller one or close off an old opening entirely, you'll probably have to deal with a scar where new material meets the old on the outside of the building. Of course, if that part of your house isn't easily viewed, or if, for instance, it faces an alley, you may not care what the exterior looks like.

Plumbing alterations are usually not recommended because of the considerable expense involved in hiring professional plumbers. But if you think you can handle the work yourself, don't be afraid to consider moving the pipes. Relocating the sink on a different wall of your kitchen could be the touch that makes your whole kitchen come together.

While you're making—or thinking about making—big changes, don't forget the wiring. Unless your house is quite new, you should replace old wiring and add new circuits wherever you can. Check the local building codes for minimum requirements, then exceed those standards if possible. Each major appliance should have its own circuit.

Planning a Smart Kitchen

Trudging around an inefficient kitchen is not good exercise. It's a waste of time and energy. It's frustrating. And it's unnecessary. What follows are some useful rules of thumb to help you design a space that will work for you.

In kitchen geometry, the work triangle is the shape that connects the sink, range, and refrigerator. Forty years ago, those three items, along with a mixer, were all there were in a typical kitchen. Even today, with all of the new appliances and gadgets and extra cooks, the triangle remains the functional center of every kitchen.

Studies have shown that in the most efficient kitchens, the three legs of this triangle will add up to at least 12 feet but no more than 23 feet. But don't worry if your intended layout doesn't fall within these guidelines. You may need to extend the triangle to preserve a view or to include a special item.

There are four basic kinds of kitchens, each with its own sort of triangle. In a *U-shaped kitchen* the triangle is compact. The U-shape lets you prepare a meal while walking the shortest distance. It works best with the refrigerator at one end of a counter—to

The U-shaped work triangle is obvious in this kitchen. The ovens reside outside the triangle.

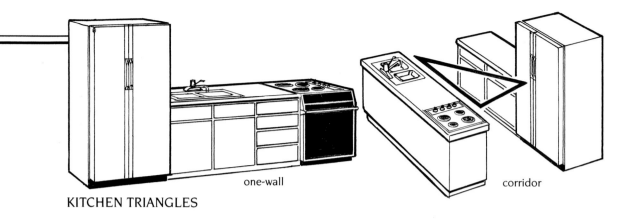

one-wall   corridor

KITCHEN TRIANGLES

keep the work area unbroken—and the sink in the center of the "U."

The *L-shaped kitchen* uses two walls of the kitchen for the three points of the triangle. This setup is well-suited for a large room, where the kitchen is also a family room. Additional counter space may lengthen one leg of the "L."

The *corridor* kitchen puts two points of the triangle on one wall and the third on the opposite. This can be a difficult kitchen to work in, especially if it is designed so that traffic flows through the middle. If the sink and range occupy the same counter, the cook will suffer fewer interruptions.

The *one-wall* kitchen is a compromise meant for tiny spaces such as in-law apartments or rental units. A one-wall kitchen can be tucked away conveniently behind closed doors, but if it includes adequate counter space, it's likely to stretch out over quite a distance and require a lot of walking. A movable table or island can improve this arrangement.

Your old kitchen and the new one you design will probably roughly conform to one of these shapes. New appliances and different layouts are changing the kitchen, causing new problems and bringing new solutions. Instead of a single, freestanding range, many modern kitchens have separate, built-in ovens and cooktops. These days, few kitchens do without a dishwasher, and many are equipped with microwave ovens and barbecue grills.

Where should you put these new elements? You can install your oven outside of the main triangle; you won't use it as often as other appliances, and most food

you bake will stay in the oven for at least 15 minutes. The microwave oven is a recent arrival on the kitchen scene and is often shunted away to a less than desirable location. Find a place for it within the triangle. Microwave cooking is fast and requires frequent checking. Consider putting the microwave near the refrigerator, since most of the food you cook in it will probably come from there.

Will your new kitchen include a barbecue grill? If it isn't part of the cooktop, the grill won't need to be in the triangle, since you won't be using it for every meal. If you're planning a two-cook kitchen, consider locating the barbecue grill in the second cook's area.

The Points of the Triangle

Nothing in your kitchen is more important than the sink. It should be close to the range and the main countertop work area. Putting those three elements all in a row on the same run of counter is a good idea, with the work area in the middle. That way, you won't have to drip water across the floor when you go from the sink to the cooktop, and party guests will be less likely to get in your way as you make last-minute preparations.

Your sink and dishwasher are bound to be close neighbors; they share a drain, and both are essential when it's time to clean up. Find a spot for the dishwasher outside of your triangle, on the side of the sink opposite the work area and the cooktop. That arrangement allows you to have the dishwasher open while you're cooking and

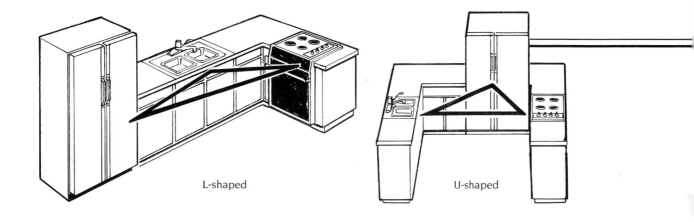

L-shaped

U-shaped

leaves room right under the work counter for storage. A dishwasher in the corner of your kitchen won't be handy; you'll have trouble reaching past its open door to high cabinets, and you won't be able to open cabinets under the counter perpendicular to it.

Today's kitchen sink often finds itself right in the middle of a popular stylistic innovation: the diagonal counter. If you install an angled counter across a corner of your room and put the sink on the angle, the dishwasher can be a problem. With the dishwasher right next to the sink in this situation, there will be no place for you to stand when the dishwasher is open. There are two solutions. You can locate the dishwasher a little farther down the counter, or you can use a recessed angled cabinet—now available from some cabinet manufacturers.

As mentioned earlier, you should take care to put your cooktop close to your sink. Avoid sections of counter and islands where there would be a foot or less of counter space on either side of the cooktop. That kind of setup leaves very little space for setting down food that's waiting to be cooked or for placing hot pots you've just removed from the heat. And don't put your cooktop right up against a high cupboard, wall oven, or refrigerator; that arrangement can make you feel claustrophobic.

With refrigerators, there are only two critical factors to keep in mind. The door should always swing out away from the triangle, and there should be at least 15 inches of counter space on the side next to the door handle.

Other Considerations

As you work out the plan for your new kitchen, give plenty of thought to two essential elements: counter space and storage. Remember your smaller appliances; no longer considered luxuries, items such as your food processor and blender need to be handy if you are to use them efficiently. Countertop appliance "garages" are wonderful, providing special spots where you can tuck away your hardware. But if the garage doors swing out, you will have to clear the counter in front of them every time you want to get at the appliances. Tambour doors, those slatted, roll-up covers, are better, since they push up out of the way.

Consider your drawers, too. Shallow ones are best. Few items take up more than 3 or 4 inches of vertical space; if your drawers are deeper than that, you're probably wasting space. And while you're looking at drawers, think about your kitchen's corners. More design mistakes are made in kitchen corners than anywhere else. (See pages 130-33.)

The best rule we know for counter space is to make sure you have plenty. Older kitchens tend to have small counters, often broken into even smaller, unusable segments. Plan plenty of counter space on the opening side of the refrigerator and on both sides of the sink and range. And if a section of your counter will have to serve a dual function—part food-preparation area, part dish-draining area, for example—try to add a few extra inches of counter.

Counter overhangs are also important. One inch will allow you to scoop spilled

Installing a sink in a recessed angled cabinet makes good use of a corner and also allows simultaneous access to the sink and a dishwasher beside it.

ingredients off the counter and into a bowl without spilling half of them down the fronts of your cabinets.

The heights of your cooks will help you decide on the heights of your counters. Thirty-six inches is standard, but many people like a higher work area. There are two basic ways to raise the counters. You can put the cabinets and the dishwasher on a platform. If you do that, be sure to tell your plumber, since your sink and dishwasher pipes will have to be extended. The other way to boost counters is to build up the tops of the cabinets before installing the countertops. This second option is less desirable, because you'll have trouble making the built-up section look presentable.

Lowering counters below 36 inches is even more difficult. Cabinets, dishwashers, and freestanding ranges all are built to that height. If you need a lower work surface, you'll probably have to have an island custom-made for you. Or consider using vanity cabinets or a table.

Endless Possibilities

You've spent years learning how to live with your kitchen's flaws. Now take a few hours to explore ways to change everything for the better. Your tools for this essential remodeling task are your scale drawing of your old kitchen, plenty of drawing and tracing paper, and an active imagination.

First, cut out templates of your sink, cooktop, refrigerator, and all of the other major components of your kitchen. Be sure to cut the templates accurately and to scale. Move the templates around on your plan until you get an arrangement you like. Then cover the plan with tracing paper, and sketch the layout. Repeat this process again and again until you've tried every conceivable configuration.

Next, try out these paper options in your real kitchen. Tape the outline of a favorite new layout on your kitchen floor. Move your big appliances around to their new positions if you can, or set up card tables or sawhorses to block out the proposed space. Then walk through the preparation of something you often cook. Does the work flow easily, or are you all over the kitchen? If you are thinking of changing the height of your counters, set up a dummy section and try that out, too. Now is the time to experiment.

Consider where you will store the kitchen tools you need every day. If you're thinking of an open kitchen with no overhead cabinets, or if you intend to replace your old walk-in pantry with an eating area, you could end up with a storage shortage. Then again, many of your present drawers and cabinets may be crowded with seldom-used items. If you can find a place in the garage for your turkey roaster and your punch bowl and can bring yourself to throw out those gadgets you haven't used in years, your would-be storage problems may solve themselves.

When Do We Start?

All of this planning and drawing and replanning and redrawing probably has you itching to get on with the job at hand. Planning is the most important part of remodeling a kitchen—or designing a kitchen from scratch. Once construction begins, changes will be expensive and time-consuming. So keep asking yourself questions until you know what you really want. Later, you'll be glad you took the time.

Lighting Strategies

Well-planned lighting makes the kitchen a safer, more efficient place to work and a more appealing living space. In devising a lighting scheme for your kitchen, remember that lighting, like many aspects of design, is subjective: One person's glare is another's gloom. There are many variables involved, including surface finishes as well as functions of different areas. That's why specific recommendations for light sources and intensity are difficult, if not impossible, to provide.

The kind of fixtures also make a difference. A fixture that hangs below the ceiling and throws light in all directions provides more illumination than a recessed fixture of a similar size.

The first rule of countertop space is to have lots of it.

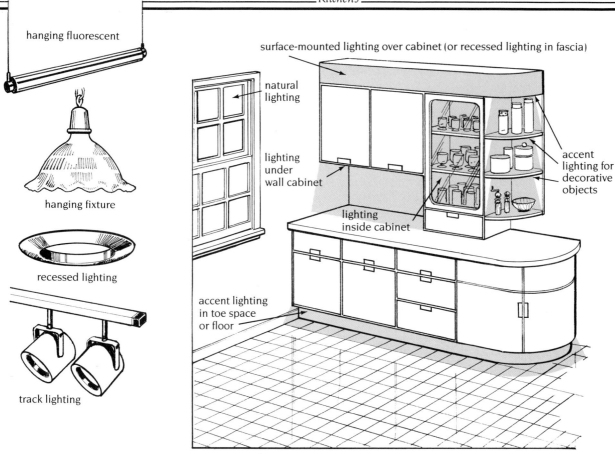

hanging fluorescent

hanging fixture

recessed lighting

track lighting

surface-mounted lighting over cabinet (or recessed lighting in fascia)

natural lighting

accent lighting for decorative objects

lighting under wall cabinet

lighting inside cabinet

accent lighting in toe space or floor

Plan for three kinds of light in your new kitchen: ambient (general illumination), task, and accent lighting.

Balancing Act

You need to be concerned about general illumination and light for jobs that don't require much visual concentration (ambient lighting). Task lighting is necessary at work stations where you must see small objects clearly. Ambient and task lighting should be well balanced. Accent lighting creates a mood or highlights objects.

The size of the kitchen greatly affects the lighting scheme. A small kitchen may require only a small ceiling fixture combined with a few undercabinet lights for the work stations. A large kitchen may combine a skylight and fixtures for ambient lighting, track lighting at work stations, and accent lighting.

Lighting sources are either fluorescent or incandescent, and each has advantages and disadvantages. Fluorescents are much more efficient. A fluorescent may consume 18 watts to produce light equal to a 75-watt incandescent. Fluorescents last longer. But only incandescents can put a certain amount of light at a certain place.

Lighting manufacturers are working on many new lamps and devices that are longer-lived and light more economically and efficiently. Small fluorescents can replace incandescent bulbs in many fixtures, and new, more efficient incandescents are also available.

Putting Light Where You Want It

Fixtures can be architectural—built in and generally less expensive—or decorative—aesthetically pleasing in their own right. Both types can be used together, though one or the other is usually emphasized.

To begin a lighting design, think about your work stations. Areas where you will be doing work requiring visual concentration need task lighting—examples are the cooking area (ranges are often lighted by a light under the hood); the sink; and stations for cutting, chopping, making bread, and similar tasks.

Task lighting can take the form of a down-pointing track or recessed light. (Use elliptical reflector lamps, commonly called ER lamps, which are focused to direct light out of the fixture, in recessed fixtures.) These work best over open counters, islands, or peninsulas. To light countertops underneath overhead cabinets, install fluorescents under the cabinets.

Installing as many dimmers and switches as you can afford gives you control over your lighting—a necessity in the kitchen. It is less expensive to dim incandescents than fluorescents. The light from one source should overlap the light from adjacent sources. Never work in shadow; it causes eyestrain and can be very dangerous in the kitchen where hot foods, sharp implements, and appliances can be hazardous as well as helpful.

Consider how the kitchen will be generally lighted. A skylight may provide enough daylight, but you'll have to install fixtures to light the room at night. The best ambient lighting is softly diffused, as when light is bounced off a light-colored ceiling.

The surface finishes in your kitchen will affect the lighting. Light colors reflect as much as 90 percent of the light that strikes them; wood or dark colors absorb as much as 90 percent. It takes less light to light a room with a light ceiling, cabinets, and walls! Light reflected from shiny surfaces may result in undesirable glare.

Finally, consider what you'd like to highlight. A wall full of decorative utensils can be washed with a fluorescent. Outstanding architectural details can be accented with an individual spot.

The color of light is as important as intensity, and the wrong color of light (such as cool white fluorescent) will make food look unappealing. Daylight is the standard against which light is measured. Incandescents, tungsten halogens, and warm white fluorescents come closest to the ideal for good color rendering.

You can hire a professional to design the lighting in your kitchen, either your architect or a lighting designer. A list of professional lighting designers in your area is available from the Illuminating Engineering Society. (See "Helpful Addresses.") Another approach is to take your plans to a lighting store, choose fixtures you like, and then allow the staff to help you place the fixtures. Most manufacturers provide brochures that give formulas for determining the exact illumination their products give in a particular setting.

A Balanced Budget

In "Questions to Answer before You Begin," one of the last questions asked you was about your budget. Now that you have a much better idea of what the possibilities are, list all the materials you'll need and all the labor you will have to pay for. The "Kitchen Budget Worksheet" (see page 140) should help you remember the essentials. When you arrive at a final total, add in a little cushion, since there are bound to be unexpected expenses. It's impossible to figure things out right down to the last dollar.

If the bottom line is more than you'd expected or can afford, you'll have to pare things down a bit. List your priorities, and see if you can at least cover them. Consider doing the job in pieces. Of course, it would be nice to see your whole new kitchen done at once, but think about whether a couple of coats of paint over the subfloor might do for a temporary floor surface. Perhaps you can live with your old dishwasher, or plumb for a new one but leave a space in the base cabinets to install it later.

The more detailed your budget, the better. There will have to be a few miscellaneous categories, but keep them to a minimum. A few trips to the local building-supply store to pick up various items, and you may find the cushion in your budget wearing down fast. Don't forget to list sales taxes and delivery charges. If you're hiring any workers who aren't licensed contractors, you'll also need to budget the cost of insurance for liability and workmen's compensation.

If the rooms surrounding your kitchen will be affected by the remodeling, include in your budget the cost of repainting walls and adding new trim. And if you're opening up exterior walls, you may decide to add new insulation.

Doing Your Own Work

Are you considering doing some of the work on your kitchen project yourself? The idea is attractive—you can save money and get a better kitchen for less. But you must be realistic about your skills and your time: Are your skills up to the demands of a complicated project? Will you have the time to do the work you want to do—or do the savings and satisfaction of doing your own work make up for the inconvenience of delay? You must also be aware that in some places building codes prohibit an unlicensed worker from doing some aspects of the work.

Before deciding that you will do work on the project yourself, take a realistic assessment of your skills. Are you capable of building cabinets or doing the wiring and plumbing? If not—or if you don't have the time—you can have these jobs done by a pro. Some less skilled jobs are easily tackled by a careful amateur—painting and tiling are good examples. Carefully research any jobs that are unfamiliar.

You may also find a contractor who will allow you to work with him, allowing you to acquire a skill and have the advantage of a professional to solve problems that come up on the job.

What role will you play in the kitchen design? If you are adding a countertop and installing a new range, you can probably function well all by yourself. For a building project that involves structural changes affecting your whole house, consider hiring an architect or kitchen designer to help you with the design, to draw plans, and to check specifications and lists of materials. At least have a professional review your plans.

Consider being the contractor for your kitchen remodeling. A general contractor is a facilitator who takes charge of the job, obtains permits, hires subcontractors, orders materials, and schedules the work. You are normally charged a percentage of the total price of the job for these services—money you can save if you do it yourself.

Taking Bids

If you are planning to do much of the work yourself, the labor part of your remodeling budget may be very small. But if a contractor will be handling the whole job, or if you will be subcontracting parts of the work, you should solicit formal bids from the people you're thinking about hiring.

Even if you know whom you are going to hire and don't need competitive bids, at least get an estimate of the costs to help you set up your budget. Unexpected problems and additional costs may crop up as the work proceeds—when the walls are opened up, for instance—but it always helps to have some kind of estimated bottom line at the outset.

If possible, have a complete set of plans available for the people bidding on the job. General sketches and a lot of hand-waving make it very difficult for anyone to present you with an accurate estimate. If you offer too few details, the contractor will probably quote you a figure higher than necessary, to cover the uncertainties.

Be sure to give each person the same information to bid on. If you neglect to tell electrician A that you want dimmers on each switch, A's bid will be less precise than that of electrician B, to whom you've given more complete information.

Make sure that you know what each bid includes. Will the contractor provide miscellaneous materials and supplies or will you have to shop for them yourself? (This kind of legwork can take many hours; if you do it, you'll save money.)

As you solicit bids, establish who will connect the range hood, the dishwasher, and other such items. On some jobs, one person will wear many hats, but on others, the role of each person is carefully set, and the carpenters won't do what they consider to be the plumber's job. Thorough planning will help you avoid confusion. If you can think of everything before work begins, you'll save time, patience, and dollars.

Specify who will clean up the work site at the end of each day. If you don't want to be crawling around under the house picking up after the plumber and electrician, say so now, when you're getting bids.

Here again you may choose to cut the cost of your project by handling the cleanup yourself. It can take up to 30 minutes of expensive hired labor every day to do this simple task. If you do it yourself, you'll also get the benefit of seeing exactly what has been done that day and how well it has been accomplished.

How Long Does It Take?

There are as many time lines for kitchen remodeling jobs as there are remodeled kitchens, but some basic guidelines apply to all. We'll use the Stones' remodeling job as an example of how long remodeling takes and how to make your job move along. The Stones' new kitchen was part of extensive remodeling that included all three levels of their house. The second level remodeling included expanding the kitchen, adding a new breakfast room, and enlarging an existing deck.

Mrs. Stone had been planning her new kitchen for years and knew exactly what she wanted: a Shaker look in her kitchen with display areas for her antiques and an efficient work triangle out of the way of traffic. She selected architect Ron Bogley to oversee and draw up the project, and Beverly Wilson, an independent kitchen designer, to help design the kitchen. The job did not have to go out to bid since Ron also acted as general contractor.

During the initial meeting of the Stones with Beverly Wilson, they discussed the Stones' basic desires, styles that appealed to them, their budget, and possible designs. Then came the necessary week or so to mull over the ideas. After this first meeting, Wilson drew up proposed designs to bring back to a second meeting. The Stones, Bogley, and Wilson worked well together and after a few months, they settled on a design.

After the contracts are signed and a retainer paid, deposits are made for custom products and cabinets. Plan one to four months for materials to arrive and the job to start. During that time do what the Stones did: Clean out the cabinets, discard unused items, prepare a workspace for the construction crew, and establish a temporary kitchen elsewhere in the house. The contractor will generally secure all permits, but check to see if this has been done. (Who gets the permits should be in the

Remodeling Time Line	
Time	Task
2 months	Gather ideas Collect examples of what you like
2 to 4 months	Interview and select architect and/or kitchen designer Meet with designer Hold second meeting with designer to approve design Hold subsequent meetings to work out design compromises Select basic design
1 to 3 months	Get bids for the job Secure a loan, if necessary Select a general contractor; sign contract; pay retainer Make required deposits (for custom products and cabinets) Get necessary permits Order materials Clean out cabinets Prepare space for workers Establish temporary kitchen Materials arrive
1 day	Tear out old kitchen
A few hours to 2 weeks	Frame in new kitchen
A few hours to many days	Complete rough plumbing work
1 to 2 days	Complete rough electrical work
6 to 8 days	Install insulation and drywall; seal; prime drywall
1 to 7 days	Install flooring
2 to 4 days	Hang cabinets; finish toe kicks and top molding
1 day	Apply final coat of paint
1 day	Trim windows and doors
1 day	Finish plumbing and electrical work
1 hour	Give the room a final inspection Move in

contract. Getting permits can take from a few minutes to two months.)

Tearing out the old kitchen usually takes a day or less. Variables include the size of the kitchen, the distance the debris has to be carried, and the number of people helping. If you are recycling woodwork or cabinets, it will take longer.

Framing of a simple job can be completed in a few hours, but as the scope of the project increases, so does the time. The Stones added on a new breakfast room, tearing out several walls, so theirs took closer to two weeks.

Rough plumbing takes anywhere from a few hours, if nothing is moved, to many days if floors above and below are involved, if delivery lines are moved, or if sinks are added or removed. Converting an all-electric kitchen to gas can add a day. The electrical rough work, which takes one to two days, comes after the plumbing. Electrical and plumbing work must be inspected before it is covered up. Usually the inspector will come soon after being called. Corrections mean delays. And, if you've had to wait for subcontractors, your schedule will move slowly.

Installing insulation is normally a straightforward job and should move fairly quickly. Usually the general contractor or carpenter installs the insulation so you won't have to wait for a subcontractor.

Some contractors do their own drywall work, but many prefer to subcontract it, so once again there is potential for delay. Allowing the various coats of joint compound to dry takes time. Each coat must dry overnight. So plan three to four days for sealing the drywall.

Painting the Stones' kitchen required about three days for a good job, which meant sealing all of the drywall so it wouldn't collect cooking odors, applying a prime coat, and finishing with two more coats to exposed areas to make the surfaces look rich. The painters put the final coat of paint on after the cabinets and floor were installed

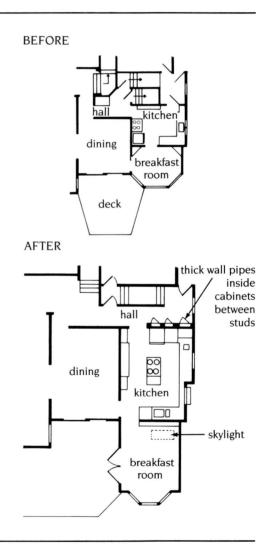

Remodeling the Stones' second level meant expanding the kitchen, adding a new breakfast room, and enlarging an existing deck.

Hints to Avoid Construction Delays

- Have your plans completely thought out and note any details that need explaining.

- Have all materials purchased and on the site, open all packages to check for damaged or incorrect items, and store the installation instructions in a notebook.

- Establish a temporary kitchen before the workers arrive and then stay out of their way.

- Prepare a large and convenient space for the workers to leave tools and supplies.

- Clear adjoining rooms and entrances of valuables and items that may be damaged by construction dust.

- Keep children and pets out of the workers' way.

- Realize that you can't control some things in construction (such as an old slow leak that's discovered when a wall is removed).

- Don't put undue pressure on workers; they will try to go as quickly as possible, especially if they are working on a fixed-price contract.

The Stones' new kitchen meant extensive remodeling, but realistic expectations in terms of time for each job and good communication among the owners, the architect, and the designer made the job move along well.

to cover marks made during installation.

The type of floor covering used determines installation time. The Stones' floor of white pine took a week, including the finishing time, during which they couldn't enter the kitchen. Installation of all but the largest tile floor takes two days. Vinyl requires only a day's time if installed by professionals.

Careful hanging of cabinets and adjustment of doors and finish details takes two to three days. Finishing the toe kicks and top molding can easily add a day, and installing window and door trim takes another.

Speed is not always important in finish work.

The plumber and electrician returned to the Stones' kitchen to hook up the appliances and lights. If your kitchen has a range hood, there will be some final sheet-metal work. Quality work up to this point makes this part go fast.

The Stones gave their kitchen a final inspection and then moved back in. Since they had packed their utensils and glassware carefully at the start of the remodeling, moving was easy. After all, this is the day they had been waiting for.

CABINETS AND COUNTERTOPS

Walk into a kitchen store, looking for cabinets, and you'll be assaulted with questions. Do you like traditional American styles, or are you interested in the newer European lines? Do you want wood cabinets—oak, ash, walnut, maple, cherry, pine—or plastic laminates? Will standard sizes work in your plan, or will your cabinets need to be custom-built? Have you considered simply refacing some of the cabinets you already have?

Your budget will have a lot to say about how you answer these questions. At the low end of the price scale, cabinets will come in fewer sizes, and you won't be able to order special variations. Still, if you can find ready-made sizes that fit your needs and spaces, you may be able to save a lot of money. As you move into the higher-priced lines, cabinets are likely to be better constructed and to offer far more options; custom-cabinet makers will fit their wares to your plan, providing cabinets that are deeper or shallower, taller or shorter than the normal offerings. Versatility inside cabinets is another important consideration, with adjustable, innovative storage systems generally costing more than simple fixed shelving.

Regardless of price, all kitchen cabinets are built from the same principal parts: the box, the face frame, the door, the drawer front, the drawer itself. (See the illustration, "Anatomy of a Kitchen Cabinet," on page 28.) The box is the cabinet's chassis, sometimes built from solid wood (plywood), but more often made of pressed board with a vinyl coating laminated to it. The thickness and density of the pressed board and the thickness of the vinyl coating will vary according to how much you pay.

The face frame is attached to the front of the box—except on European-style cabinets, which don't have separate face frames. The face frame is the part you see; the doors are hinged to it, the drawers slide through it, and the drawer front rests against it. On more expensive cabinets, the face frame will be doweled to the box, while economy models will probably be fastened together with a nail gun. The doors and the drawer fronts will be made of the same material as the face frame.

The style and composition of the face frames, drawer fronts, and cabinet doors establish the "look" of your new kitchen. But when you're picking out your cabinets,

26

look beyond surface charm. Check inside the cabinet to see how well it's put together. Are the interior surfaces smooth? Does the bottom rail of the face frame line up with the bottom shelf? (If it doesn't, there will be a lip to trap crumbs when you try to wipe out the cupboard.) Can the shelves be adjusted up and down to fit your needs? Are the hinges sturdy and the drawer glides strong enough to stand up to heavy use?

Base cabinets are the ones that fit under your countertops. Most are built to fairly regular dimensions: 24 inches deep and 34½ inches high—so that a 1½-inch-thick counter will make the total height the standard 36 inches. Where base cabinets do vary is in width. The narrowest you can get is 9 inches wide, but from there, sizes build up in 3-inch increments.

Base cabinets up to a width of 24 or 27 inches (depending on the manufacturer) will have only one door; a cabinet from 24 or 27 inches to 48 inches wide will have two doors. In some two-door cabinets, the center stile is attached to one of the doors to allow better access to the interior. Base cabinets typically have one drawer with a cupboard below, but you can also get two drawers above a shorter cupboard, or base units with three or four drawers. Unless you're buying custom cabinets, though, you'll have to work with standard drawer depths.

Corner cabinets are a special kind of base cabinet. In order to make good use of otherwise wasted space, a corner cabinet will usually be fitted with one of three styles of lazy Susan (revolving shelves). Some corner cabinets are made with a diagonal door, with a complete lazy Susan inside. Others come with right-angled doors attached to the revolving shelves; this configuration can be dangerous since it's easy to catch fingers in the door as it comes around again. The third style has right-angled doors that open away from a wedge-shaped lazy Susan.

The sink base is another sort of base cabinet. Although it can't have a full top drawer—the sink would get in the way—it usually has a false drawer front that maintains the horizontal line of the rest of the cabinets. But you don't have to waste the few inches of space between the drawer front and the sink. It's possible to get a sink base with a tilt-down front that hides a rack big enough to hold sponges and scrubbers.

Most *upper cabinets* are approximately 12 inches deep, but many different heights, from 12 to 42 inches, are available. If you plan to put an upper cabinet above your sink, consider installing a short, high one—perhaps with a shallow shelf below it—so you won't feel cramped when you work at the sink.

The cupboard over the refrigerator is another special case. Since a refrigerator tends to be relatively deep, it's wise to install a deep cabinet above it. Otherwise, you'll have trouble reaching the cabinet and may find yourself stacking things on top of the refrigerator—things that will have to be moved before you can open the doors to the cabinet. One good solution is to use a 24-inch-deep cabinet that's tall enough to provide vertical storage for cookie sheets and serving trays.

Upper cabinets seldom extend more than 7 feet above the floor, although it's possible to go 8 feet or even higher. But rows of very high cabinets may be inaccessible and can tend to overwhelm a room.

Tall cabinets—cupboards that stretch from the floor almost to the ceiling—are generally built to be 7 feet tall; if you want your cabinets to go higher, you'll probably have to order a special 12-inch-high box to fit on top of a standard tall cabinet. This type of cabinet may house a wall oven or function as a pantry unit or broom closet. Sometimes even refrigerators are hidden away in tall cabinets for a built-in appearance. Most tall cabinets are at least 18 inches wide, although several cabinet lines now feature an expensive but very handy 12-inch-wide version with pull-out storage. Tall cabinets, in general, come with quite an assortment of storage options. And some high-priced cabinet lines offer a tall corner cabinet that solves the tricky corner problem very nicely. An angled door provides access to the entire roomy interior.

The Refacing Option

If you like the layout of your old kitchen and the basic configuration of the cabinets, refacing the cabinets can give you a new look at a considerable discount. Refacing usually involves removing the doors and drawer fronts but leaving the face frames in place. The frames are then covered with a wood veneer or plastic laminate, new doors are attached with new hinges, and new drawer fronts are attached to the old drawer box. Install new hardware, and your revitalized kitchen is quickly complete.

ANATOMY OF A CABINET

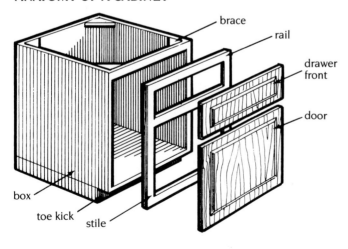

brace

rail

drawer front

door

box

toe kick

stile

European-style cabinetry has full-overlay doors (no hinges visible), which create a sleek, contemporary look.

Types of Cabinets

The 1970s brought European cabinets to the American market. Once considered a fad, they have become big sellers, and more and more American manufacturers are adding the European look to their lines. Don't let the name confuse you. The style is European no matter where they are made—Germany or Pennsylvania.

Several striking differences set European-style cabinets apart from their American cousins. European-style cabinets don't have separate face frames. The door, which

29

In American-style cabinetry (traditional), hinges and the face frame around the edge of the doors are visible. These cabinets and the facing for the refrigerator are light oak.

Nearly anything is possible in kitchen cabinetry. This cabinet, which follows the oriental style, has black-lacquered maple doors with designs brushed on in gold lacquer.

can and European styles. From the exterior, a hybrid cabinet looks like a European-style cabinet with flush doors and no hinges showing. The cabinet has a face frame like that of the American style.

Assemble-Yourself Cabinets

You can save money when you work with a carpenter building your house, and

TYPES OF CABINETS

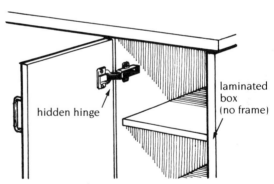

Traditional or American

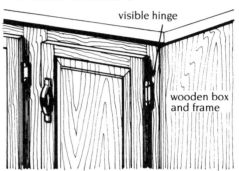

European Style

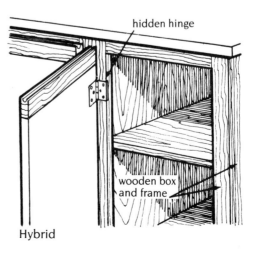

Hybrid

is hinged right to the box and covers the entire front of it, is called a *full-overlay door.* A European drawer front works the same way. This gives European-style cabinets a much cleaner look, but you have to be careful not to crowd them into corners, since their doors need extra room to open. The box of an American cabinet is made of wood, whereas the box of a European-style cabinet is constructed of laminated particle board.

European-style cabinets are installed after the finished floor has been laid; American cabinets go in before the floor, with the flooring sometimes carried up into the toe kick as covering.

The toe kick on European-style cabinets is higher, which means you won't have to bend down as far to reach bottom shelves. But the toe-kick space doesn't have to go to waste. You can order special drawers that slide into the toe kick; these drawers are good places to store seldom-used items.

Where clever storage systems are concerned, European cabinets were the state of the art, but American manufacturers have quickly caught up.

There is also a cabinet type that is called a *hybrid,* a combination of the Ameri-

31

Using side-mounted hinges by Grass America, the craftsman who made these cabinets (of red birch with rosewood stripes and walnut handles) has hidden the face frames behind the doors.

The door panels in these cabinets are of stained glass—proving that cabinets can be made of material other than wood and laminates.

More than anything else, cabinetry sets the tone of a kitchen. Here the high-gloss, red-lacquered cabinets with polished chrome-plated trim and pulls complement the mirror backsplash and granite countertop.

33

The joy of knockdown cabinets is that you can take them with you when you move. These cabinets are in the European style and are plastic laminate with wood trim.

the same logic follows when you help out the cabinetmaker. Instead of buying ready-made cabinets at today's high prices, you can pay less if you construct them yourself from kits or knockdown (KD) components.

And you won't be sacrificing quality or style. The cabinets are made from fine grades of wood or sturdy laminates. A wide variety of styles are available: One kit manufacturer has 24 door styles available, and the KD cabinets offer an enormous selection from traditional American to exotic European. Assembly for both kit and KD cabinets is easy and fast. You will need some basic tools, such as a screwdriver and a hammer, but only minimal carpentry skills are necessary. Easy-to-understand instructions accompany these assemble-yourself cabinets.

Kit Cabinets

Kit cabinets can be custom-designed for your kitchen. One kit company, Cabinetmaster (see "Helpful Addresses"), will provide design assistance for your kitchen remodeling. There's an extra fee for the advice, which varies according to the size of your kitchen. Along with the design help, you'll see a watercolor rendition of what your kitchen will look like. The cabinets are available in oak, birch, cherry, and maple, and with a choice of 24 door styles. The cabinet joints are precision-machined, making these kits easy to assemble. According to Cabinetmaster, two inexperienced people can assemble 15 of the kit cabinets in seven hours. After assembly, you glue the joints for a permanent bond. The application of your choice of finish completes the job. Cabinetmaster will do custom finishing and match existing colors for an extra fee.

KD Cabinets

KD cabinets are different from kit cabinets since they're less permanent. The joints aren't glued like kit cabinets, so it's easy to knock down the cabinets and take them with you when you move, a common practice in Europe. You get a break on price with KD cabinets, because retailers and manufacturers save on freight and space and the cabinets are less likely to be damaged in storage. One KD company, Famco

European cabinetmakers lead the pack in ingenious storage systems. The slides for these appliance garages are from Austria.

and -built kitchens in laminate, pine, walnut, or oak. The cabinets are available unfinished, too. KD kitchen cabinets are fairly new to this country, but will soon be more readily available in home centers and kitchen stores.

Behind the Cabinet Door

Gaining more storage space is a major goal in most kitchen remodeling. However,

Drawer inserts for cooking utensils keep tools close at hand but out of sight.

Distributor (see "Helpful Addresses"), makes European-style cabinets designed for efficient storage capacity. The laminate surface inside and out provides for easy maintenance. You can choose the hardware for these cabinets since screw holes are only partially prebored. Another KD manufacturer, American Marketing and Management (see "Helpful Addresses"), distributes a wide variety of European-designed

The wire racks in this pantry easily store scores of cans for quick access.

most kitchens already have underutilized storage space lurking behind cabinet doors and drawer fronts. A variety of built-in storage systems can dramatically increase kitchen storage.

European cabinet manufacturers have long been adept at designing ingenious storage options for their cabinets, and Americans are fast catching up. As a result, there are many space-saving possibilities on the market. Custom cabinetmakers are also adept at devising specially built drawers and storage units.

Storage space within cabinets greatly improves by simply fitting out cabinets with pull-out shelves, rather than stationary ones. In some European-style cabinets, these shelves are adjustable up and down within the cabinet, which allows greater flexibility in storage. A combination of slide-out shelves and bins is particularly handy.

Another common option for retrofitting cabinets is to use some of the storage systems available at many home-supply stores. For example, there are a variety of plastic lazy Susans and racks that you can simply screw into kitchen cabinets and set into drawers. Racks for hanging wine glasses from their bases or for stacking plates can better utilize space within wall cabinets where shelves can't be moved up or down to save space.

Lazy Susans are a good solution to using otherwise-wasted space within corner cabinets. Lazy Susans are available from cabinet manufacturers, or they can be built to order by a cabinetmaker. Shelves that swing out from a corner cabinet on a vertical plastic axis are sold at hardware stores and home-supply centers for retrofitting existing corner cabinets.

Another ingenious storage idea is a slide-out wastebasket mount for under-the-sink installation in a cabinet next to the sink. Some hold a standard-sized wastebasket, while others are wire frames within which a plastic garbage bag hangs.

A variety of drawer inserts improves storage within drawers. Some of these are simply updated versions of cutlery baskets, sized to organize the storage of spatulas, whips, and other kitchen utensils. Slotted racks in a drawer store knives conveniently

This pantry, just 12 inches deep, stores lots of cans and dry goods, but nothing gets lost. The cabinet is not wide enough to impede traffic.

but away from children. Custom-fitted utensil drawers can be created using parting stop, a molding commonly available at lumberyards, or similar thin wooden strips. A deep drawer with vertical dividers is a handy place to store lids for pots and pans; a very deep drawer may accept cookie sheets and other baking pans.

37

Leaded-glass panels with wildflowers let you see what's stored *behind* the cabinet doors.

These wedge-shaped drawers, lined with copper, have hammered-copper lids.

This floor-to-ceiling corner cabinet conceals two lazy Susans that provide lots of hidden storage.

Wrinkle-free storage for tablecloths is possible with these unique racks.

Roll-out drawers below a cooktop provide handy storage for spices, pots, and pans.

Open Storage

If you visit a restaurant kitchen, you're likely to find a work table right in front of the range with plates stacked on a shelf above it, stock pots on a shelf underneath, and saucepans and skillets hanging from a huge rack overhead. If there's a shelf above the range, it will be stacked with more saucepans, baking tins, and utensils.

There's a very good reason why restaurants store pots, pans, and utensils this way. For them, time is money. A restaurant can't afford to have workers hunting for the tools of their trade. Open storage of all kinds—shelves, countertop storage, and various racks—keeps everything visible and close at hand so it can be located quickly and with a minimum of wasted motion.

Open storage has exactly the same virtues at home. Busy home cooks appreciate being able to see and to grab the exact item they need just as much as the pros do.

Some cabinetry combines the best of both open and closed storage. Cookbooks and wine glasses are readily at hand, and antique glassware is on display. The small drawers contain recipes and treats for the children.

Here cooking utensils, spices, and appliances are stored where they are used—in the open.

40

Knives stuck into a slotted rack beside a chopping block provide the perfect work station for serious cooking.

Being able to lift a pot from a rack rather than retrieve it from a drawer may mean that you don't have to stop and clean messy hands first—or root through the drawer to find just the pot desired.

Shirley Cavallo, whose kitchen is featured in "Gallery: A Tour of Fine Kitchens," relies extensively on open storage. She has a simple dictum to explain this preference: "If it's hidden, you don't use it. I use my equipment."

In the Cavallo kitchen, pots hang from ceiling beams. Knives are stored where they are used—they jut from a slotted rack mounted on the side of the chopping block and are stuck blade-first into knife blocks set on the counter at other work stations. Jars of herbs sit on shelves. Other pots, pans, and utensils are stored on shelves or countertops convenient to their place of use. Even the food processor, blender, and twin KitchenAid mixers sit on the countertop, ready for action.

One of the drawbacks of open storage is that items stored in the open get dirty if they are not used. They also can look messy if unorganized. In the Cavallo kitchen, cooking tools of all sorts are used frequently, if not daily, and are always clean. Shirley Cavallo also knows the importance of organization; her kitchen is orderly despite the large number of utensils hanging in her kitchen.

An additional consideration when selecting an open storage system is that items displayed in the open automatically make a design statement. To some people, this is a distinct advantage. Pots and pans, whether hung from an overhead rack or on the wall, look functional, and this appeals to many people. If they are heavy-duty copper or otherwise commercial in style, they betoken a serious cook. Pottery, stemware, dinnerware, and cups are often attractive enough to be displayed openly in almost any kitchen.

Open shelving can be a particularly effective means of storage in a small kitchen. Using various open storage systems means gaining space required for the clearance necessary to open cabinet doors and drawers.

If you like the idea of using some open storage in your kitchen, you can combine open storage systems, such as racks, with closed cabinets. A cabinet with a glass front can simulate an open shelf as a place to store pottery and elegant stemware.

Hanging copper pots and pans look functional but are also decorative.

The New Laminates

America's kitchen designers have developed a love affair with laminates. It's easy to see why. Today's laminates come in more colors, patterns, and textures than ever before. What's more, product improvements make laminates an increasingly versatile finish material. So, if your kitchen is old-fashioned and in need of an update, you might consider installing a decorative laminate.

Don't let terminology confuse you. Many people refer to plastic laminates as Formica. The fact is that the Formica Corporation is the company that first developed plastic laminates and gave its product the name of Formica. Formica is the largest manufacturer of laminates in the world, but there are many others now that make laminates. (See "Helpful Addresses.") So, don't think of Formica as a generic term for plastic laminates. It is just one of many.

Decorative laminates spring from humble origins. A sheet of laminate is actually made of paper—layer upon layer of paper, impregnated with plastic resin, then sandwiched together under great pressure and heat until the layers bond chemically into a single sheet. The surface appearance of the laminate comes from the color, texture, or pattern printed on the top layer. A sheet of plastic laminate is a kind of veneer; it must be glued to a supporting structure of plywood or particle board. Laminates can cover counters, cabinets, tables, even walls, providing a finish that's beautiful, durable, and easy to maintain.

Before you go shopping for a laminate, consider these design tips.

Color

Today's laminates come in virtually hundreds of colors. Pale neutrals, including various shades of white, almond, gray, and beige are still popular, as are pastels. But if you're interested in something more striking, there are also dark neutrals—dark grays, coffees, and blacks—vivid primaries, and bright jewel tones available.

Many laminate companies offer color-coordinated palettes to help you mix and match laminates of different shades. One company, Laminart (see "Helpful Addresses"), has even developed a color system, Isochromatics, that assures a perfect match no matter which colors you choose. According to the company, all of the colors in the system are created with the exact same degree of brightness, so that there is never a conflict in brightness as there is with many traditional color combination systems.

With so many choices in the laminate palette, it shouldn't be difficult for you to find one that will suit your color scheme. But if your new laminates will be part of a larger renovation, consider this helpful design trend: Several laminate makers have joined forces with carpeting, wallpaper, and fabric manufacturers to develop groups of color-coordinated products. One such program, available through interior designers, is the Coordinated Resources Program by Walker Group, which involves laminates from the Nevamar Corporation, carpets from Karastan, and fabrics from Scalamandre.

Patterns

Gold specks on a white background were yesterday's fashion statement. Today

Laminates are available in any color you can imagine. Count the colors in this kitchen, designed by Mark Simon. Twelve colors, as Simon says, "play off one another for visual delight."

Bands of color in this laminate kitchen with a country look give the room a light and open feeling.

you can get shadow-checks, pinstripes, and woodgrains, along with granite, marble, slate, and leather look-alikes. There are patterns that imitate linen, homespun, corduroy, and flannel; sleek, mirrored metallics; and basketweave, cane, and reed looks.

You can also create your own patterns by combining different laminates. For example, you can create a sleek, high-tech look by using a plain laminate in one of the new grays and inlaying it with a stripe of silver metallic laminate.

New Ways to Use Laminates

Product improvements have made modern laminates increasingly versatile. One of the most exciting developments is the solid-color laminate. With conventional laminates, only the top layer of the paper sandwich is

43

Laminate cabinetry in bright colors makes a striking statement. These cabinets, laminate inside and outside, are in the European style and have oak edge banding and pulls.

printed with a color or pattern. Underneath, there is kraft paper, responsible for the dark seam usually evident along the edge of a laminate countertop. But today you can get laminates with color that goes all of the way through the core. When applied with a colorless glue, like white glue or uncolored contact cement, these solid-core laminates can be used to create a virtually seamless countertop. Solid-color laminates can also be layered to create striped edges, routed, beveled, engraved, or inlaid with wood along the edges for a decorative effect.

Today's thinner laminates can be shaped and sculpted for special effects. Some can even be curved or radiused. Many come grooved for use as tracked tambour cabi-

net doors. This kind of pliability makes the material suitable for furniture, columns, pilasters, and other fine architectural details.

Hardware

More and more manufacturers are introducing hardware lines that emphasize bright, cheerful colors and sleek, new shapes. Because of its clean designer looks and the wide range of colors available, laminate pairs beautifully with the latest looks in faucets, knobs, pulls, and handles. Consider pairing a laminate in a primary color with a strong red or clear yellow handle. If you like the European look, a white laminate with a white plastic handle or a light-colored wood handle is the way to go. Want something futuristic? Think about one of the new lavender-grays, inlaid with silver metallic laminate set off by silver knobs.

Be creative: Try outlining a particularly nice handle with an inlaid stripe of laminate in a contrasting color. And look into the possibility of using laminate itself as a handle. You can layer up sheets of laminates and groove or route indentations in the laminate "plywood" to make your own attractive cabinet pulls.

Durability

New laminates are more durable than their predecessors. You can get surface coatings that resist scuff marks, dull patches, and other signs of wear etched into laminate surfaces by sliding objects, acids, and solvents. Solid-core laminates, which are often more brittle and more easily marked than conventional laminates protected by one of the new coatings, nevertheless appear to age more slowly because the color extends through, making nicks and scratches less obvious.

Where you use your laminate will help determine what kind to buy. You'll need a thicker laminate—0.05 inch—for horizontal surfaces; for vertical installations, a 0.028-inch thickness will suffice. A high-gloss finish will probably hold up on a vertical surface, but a matte finish is better for the tops of counters and tables, where the laminate is bound to suffer more wear and tear.

Maintaining your laminate countertop or laminate-veneered cabinets is easy. Just clean with a cloth or sponge and all-purpose household cleaner and water. Avoid the use of abrasive cleaners or pads and strong acid, ammonia, or other solvents, and your

Versatile, modern laminates create seamless countertops or ones with special edge treatments. ColorCore has five custom edge treatments (clockwise from the top left: wood ogee, wood chamfer, pinstripe, rounded-edge, and self-edge).

elegant new look will brighten your kitchen for many years to come.

Doing-It-Yourself

You may be able to install your own laminate cabinets, depending on the complexity of your project and how handy you are with tools. Most laminates can be worked with conventional woodworking tools or metalworking equipment. Some manufacturers offer how-to instructions.

Because laminates are more often specified by professional designers and architects than by homeowners, you might have some trouble finding a wide selection at your local home center or hardware store. If this is the case, check the Yellow Pages for the names of laminate distributors, or write directly to manufacturers.

Counter Points

There is no single counter material that's perfect for every kitchen. Each kind has its advantages and disadvantages. Plastic laminates are the most popular choice and probably the most versatile. The selection of colors is endless, and for those who don't like the material's characteristic dark edge lines, Formica's ColorCore and Wilsonart's Solicor (manufactured by the Ralph Wilson Plastics Corporation) have surface colors that go clear through.

Installing plastic laminate counters can be do-it-yourself projects. You can make your own laminate counter by gluing the plastic sheets to a piece of particle board. For common sizes, many lumberyards have precut pieces complete with backsplash and front edge; you just cut it to length and install it.

The major disadvantage to laminates is that you can't cut on them without damaging the surface, and a hot pot will scorch the plastic. With laminate counters, you'll need to keep cutting boards handy and have a tile or some other kind of heat-resistant surface next to your cooktop. Or

Red tile covers the countertop and backsplash. Decorative tile on the backsplash and an edging of birch on the countertop provide the right accents.

you can have a heat-resistant surface inset in the laminate.

Corian, a beautiful, but expensive, counter material, is a synthetic product made by E. I. Du Pont de Nemours & Company. You can also get a sink made of Corian, if you'd like the look of a one-piece molded surface. Corian can be cut fairly easily with a saw, but you may want to leave this job to the pros. Although very strong once installed, Corian is flexible when unsupported; make a wrong move, and you may find yourself with two pieces instead of one. For accent color, you could edge Corian with wood or plastic strips glued to the edge sandwich-style.

If you try to cut on Corian, you'll dull your knife blade, but the scratches can be sanded out, along with minor scorch marks.

Probably every good cook has had dreams of endless butcher-block counters; not only would such a kitchen be full of built-in cutting boards, it would also look very warm and functional. But wood is a poor choice for around the sink—wood and water are natural enemies—and near the range you would need a buffer strip of some heat-resistant material to set pots on. Butcher block should be treated with oil to keep it from drying out. Sections of your butcher-block counter that will come into contact with food should be protected with FDA-approved mineral oil. Depending on how you use a butcher-block counter, you'll need to sand it down every so often to remove scars and refresh its appearance. For weekly sanitizing, you can use a solution of 1 tablespoon of Clorox in a quart of warm water. Wipe the counters and then dry them.

Marble and granite both make beautiful counter surfaces. They're cold and hard, perfect for making pastry and some kinds of candy. Many cooks like to include a stone surface in their baking areas. Marble will etch if it comes in contact with high-acid food such as lemon juice.

Another hard surface, ceramic tile, has long been a favorite for counters, although it does have its drawbacks. It's noisy to work on, unforgiving when a dish is dropped, and should not be used as a cutting surface. Two distinct advantages are that tile is available in a staggering number of styles and

Warm, rich-looking butcher block provides a home for this cooktop. At the bottom of the photo, note the ceramic tile that protects the countertop from hot pans.

that installing a tile counter is within reach of most do-it-yourselfers. Many kinds of tile that couldn't stand up to the beating a floor would get work fine on a counter. To give it a smooth look, you can cap the edge of the tile counter with more tile or wood strips. In many kitchens, the tile of the counter is continued up the wall to the cabinets, making it the major decorating statement for the entire room. And since tile can take

47

Countertops

Material	Advantages	Disadvantages	Care
Butcher block	Warm, functional appearance; can be used for cutting surface; acquires patina over years of use; can be installed by careful homeowner	Expensive; will scorch; can be damaged by water, so not recommended for installation around sinks; stains readily; not grease-resistant; scratches easily	Wipe clean with damp cloth; sanitize weekly; needs periodic oiling for long-term protection; scratches and minor scorch marks can be sanded off
Ceramic tile	Tremendous selection of colors, textures, and finishes; extremely hard and durable; completely waterproof and stain- and heat-resistant; damaged tiles are easily replaced; can be installed by careful homeowner	Breakables shatter when dropped on tile; can't be used for cutting surface; noisy to work on; limited choice of grout colors; grout stains and breaks out	Clean with water and all-purpose household cleaner; scrub grout with small brush; wipe off after cleaning; steel-wool pads will scratch some tile; some tile can be cleaned with a nylon pad; check manufacturer's product claims before cleaning
Corian	Solid color all the way through; durable; hard; stain- and grease-resistant; easy to work; can be glued and routed for interesting edge treatments; strong; sink can be molded into countertop for seamless appearance	Limited color selection; will scorch; can't be used for cutting surface—dulls knives; expensive; Du Pont recommends that hot pots *not* be set on Corian	Wipe off with detergent or cleanser; polish with household cleaner and Scotch-Brite pad; scratches and minor scorch marks can be sanded off
Metals (stainless steel, copper)	Durable; sanitary; easy to clean; stainless steel matches commercial appliances; copper has a warm appearance	Both have soft surfaces and scratch easily; can't be used for cutting surface; finish dulls easily; streaks show; must be custom-fabricated; expensive	Stainless steel wipes clean; disinfect with ammonia; polish with the grain using a low-abrasive cleanser and nylon pad, or use stainless-steel polish; copper must be polished fre-

Tile is not a good cutting surface. Inlaying a cutting board solves the problem.

water and heat, it's a good choice for next to your cooktop and sink.

There are a few other options for kitchen counters, all of them less common and most likely more expensive. Slate is dense and extremely hard. Metal countertops fit into the decor of some kitchens. Stainless steel is sanitary and easy to clean and therefore abounds in commercial kitchens. Copper has a warm glow. Both stainless steel and copper are heat resistant but do not offer good cutting surfaces.

If you're not satisfied with any one of the particular choices of countertop material, you might consider insetting different materials into your countertops. For example, you might choose laminates for most of your countertops but inset tiles around the range and around a section of butcher block in an island.

Finally, if you'd like to change the appearance of your kitchen but don't have a lot of money, consider simply changing your countertops. Such a change is quick to make and can change the look of the room dramatically. Best of all, installing most of the popular countertops is a simple project for a careful do-it-yourselfer.

Material	Advantages	Disadvantages	Care
Metals (continued)			quently; lacquering will protect a copper finish
Plastic laminates	Versatile—can be used for vertical and horizontal surfaces and for curves; wide range of colors, textures, and finishes; resists stains, abrasions, and grease; relatively inexpensive; many lumberyards and building-supply companies stock laminate tops in common sizes; can be installed by careful homeowner ColorCore and Solicor offer the above advantages and are a solid color through and through; scratches are less apparent and black joint and edge lines are eliminated	Not heat-resistant; can't be used for cutting surface; will dull and chip over time; black lines at edges and joints, except with ColorCore and Solicor	Clean with a damp cloth and soap or liquid detergent; never use abrasive cleaners; remove stains with alcohol, lacquer thinner, or paint thinner
Stone (granite, marble, slate)	Beautiful; distinctive color variation in marble; granite and slate vary less; cool surface—particularly good for pastry and candy making; slate and granite are very hard and durable, stain-resistant, and waterproof	Expensive; edge treatments limited; can't be used for cutting surface; marble is porous and stains easily; acids are a particular problem; extremely heavy; must be custom-fabricated	Granite and slate wipe clean. Marble should be sealed; when used as food preparation surface, seal surface with salad oil and wipe up spills with sudsy water; when not used as a surface for food preparation, use a commercial sealer and follow care instructions

Islands and Peninsulas

Peninsulas, sections of countertop that jut out into a room and are attached to a counter at one end, and islands, which are freestanding, play a big role in kitchen design, and for good reason.

A strategically placed island or peninsula can shrink a large kitchen down to size, making the work area more efficient. In a small kitchen, a movable island can provide extra storage and additional counter space.

But islands and peninsulas perform many other functions. They can channel traffic flow where you want it, away from the major work stations in the kitchen. They can serve as homes for a cooktop or range, a location for a sink, or even house an undercounter refrigerator. They can function as a serving area for buffets or a staging area for sit-down dining, as a counter for informal meals, and as a place for guests or family to sit and kibitz with the cook.

Islands and peninsulas can be as simple as a chopping block in the center of the kitchen or a work table set against a wall. Or they can be permanent with plumbing, wiring, and gas lines to service built-in appliances.

This sink-equipped island effectively keeps traffic out of the cook's way and makes an efficient work triangle.

This peninsula serves as a buffet (the countertop of tile beside the range is good for hot dishes) and as a place for guests to gather to watch the cook at work. It does extra duty as a storage place for the owners' considerable cookbook collection.

This island has multiple functions: It's home to a cooktop; it has additional storage space; it makes the work triangle more compact; and its curves echo those in other parts of the kitchen.

Even a small island can contain several work stations. The fact that the island is accessible from all sides means that several people can work at once. For example, an island for food preparation may contain a sink, which is accessible from two sides, as well as butcher blocks. Or an island may house a cooktop surrounded by tile surfaces and an area for food preparation. Islands should contain toe-kick space on all four sides.

In some kitchens, two small islands can work better than one large island. Each island can be devoted to a specific task, allowing both flexibility and space for several people to work at once.

Islands or peninsulas can make the work triangle significantly more efficient by eliminating steps and allowing the range and refrigerator to be located on one wall and the sink on an island or peninsula. An island or peninsula often works well with U- or L-shaped kitchen floor plans.

A peninsula can serve as a visual and functional separation between areas, defining the kitchen as a space but allowing people in the kitchen to communicate with those in an adjacent room.

There are some consequences of adding an island or peninsula to a kitchen. Storage will be reduced if there are no cabinets over the island or peninsula. Cabinets that are installed over a peninsula should be reinforced at the top. Special arrangements are necessary for running services to an island. Ranges or cooktops set in islands often have down-draft ventilation instead of ventilation hoods.

These problems can be circumvented easily enough. Down-draft ranges, such as the Jenn-Air, are easily mounted in a freestanding island. In a large kitchen, an island might be made extra wide for additional undercounter storage, or there may be room for a small pantry to house the items that might otherwise be placed in overhead cabinets. Cabinets mounted in a peninsula are particularly handy if access is available from both sides.

Sinks and Faucets

Once upon a time, you could buy either a single sink or a double sink or maybe a deep laundry sink with a drainboard cover. You could get white porcelain enamel or stainless steel. Life was simple then. Now it's not so simple but a lot more fun. These days, there are hundreds of combinations of sink sizes, colors, and materials from which to choose.

When you start browsing through kitchen-sink catalogs, you'll find several different dimensions listed. The outside dimensions of the sink unit are usually written showing length (front to back) and width. Rectangular bowl sizes will be listed in the same way, along with the bowl depth; circular sinks will show the diameter, then the depth.

Bowl sizes, as well as the kind and number of bowls included in a particular sink unit, offer options to suit almost anyone's needs. There are at least ten different single-sink bowl sizes, ranging from 12 by 12 inches up to 16 by 28 inches. Double-sink units usually house two bowls of the same size—14 by 17 inches is the most common—but there are six or more other sizes available. You can also get two-bowl sinks with one bowl that's twice the size of the other. Typically, you would connect a garbage disposal to the smaller sink and leave the larger one

White and beige are the most popular colors for sinks, but a rainbow of colors is available. This porcelain enamel, cast-iron sink is vibrant in red. Note the matching red grout.

Stainless steel is a good alternative to porcelain enamel sinks. The adjustable-height faucet is convenient when washing big pots.

free for washing big items, such as your roasting pan.

And in case two bowls aren't enough for you, there are now three-bowl units put together in a number of different configurations. Often, one of the bowls will be small and shallow, and the ledge for the faucets may be located toward one end of the unit, leaving more room for larger bowls at the other end.

Round sinks are another new twist in kitchen accoutrement. Most of these units consist only of a round bowl with a narrow lip that fits down onto the counter. Round sinks don't usually include faucet ledges; faucets for round sinks are attached through the countertop instead. You can install two round sinks side by side, but you'll have to be careful when you swing your spout across from one to the other. If you don't turn off the water first, you'll flood your counter.

When it comes to materials, you still have two basic sink choices: stainless steel or porcelain enamel. But there are important variations to consider. Stainless-steel sinks come in 18-, 20-, or 22-gauge thicknesses; the lower the gauge number, the heavier the metal, and the less "tinny" the sink will sound. Shiny stainless-steel sinks are difficult to keep perfect, since every water spot will show. An easier alternative is a brushed or matte finish.

Porcelain enamel sinks are made with an enamel finish baked onto steel or cast iron. The latter is more durable and more expensive. White porcelain enamel sinks

are still available and quite popular, but the rainbow of sink colors keeps growing and changing.

Since we've moved beyond the days of the simple sink, this very necessary kitchen item has become an important decorative element in the kitchen. So, in addition to porcelain enamel and stainless-steel sinks, you can choose from copper, brass, Corian, and acrylic ceramic sinks.

Faucets

Faucets are changing at least as fast as everything else in the kitchen. Faucet prices start at about $50 and go up to $300 and beyond—a considerable range that suggests the amazing variety on the market. Chrome-plated brass fixtures, once your only choice, now share the stage with solid-brass faucets and others finished in bright enameled colors. Many faucets still have separate controls for hot and cold water, but single-knob or lever controls are becoming increasingly popular. Spouts come in all sizes and shapes, some quite unusual. You can get faucets with hose and spray attachments built into the spouts, and some sinks come drilled with extra holes that let you install soap or hand-cream dispensers next to the faucet. There are even faucets that are activated by infrared sensors when you put

This sink is installed flush with ceramic tile for easy clean-up and food preparation in a recessed area.

A Corian sink and countertop in almond is the perfect match for a brass, gooseneck faucet.

This diagonal sink arrangement has two different-sized bowls with a draining area in the back.

your hands under them. That way you "turn them on" without having to touch them—an advantage for a cook with sticky fingers.

As you sift through all of the possibilities, keep two concerns in mind. The spout you choose should be high enough to accommodate a tall pot, and the handles should be easy to manipulate. Those handles that look like oversized golf balls surely were designed by a noncook. When you have chocolate frosting all over your fingers or have been cutting up a chicken, you will prefer a faucet you can turn on and regulate with as little hand contact as possible. Many people find a single-lever faucet to be best.

Pure Water on Tap

It looks clean, it tastes clean, and it smells just fine—but is that glass of water from your kitchen tap truly fit to drink? A growing number of Americans are having doubts about their drinking water as more and more contaminants are being discovered in our water supplies. Some of those impurities, such as the minerals that constitute "hardness," present no particular health threat. Some contaminants are only potentially harmful in large quantities. But others are unsafe at any level.

Traditional forms of municipal water treatment are, in general, doing a good job of filtering out sand, dirt, algae, bacteria, and viruses. But municipal treatment plants are less well-equipped to remove some of today's industrial and agricultural pollutants—dissolved inorganic substances like cadmium, lead, mercury, and nitrites, as well as organic contaminants such as pesticides, herbicides, and industrial solvents. Laws setting maximum permissible levels of some contaminants have been on the books since 1974. They are, however, difficult to enforce—and the list of potentially harmful substances they regulate is far from exhaustive. Furthermore, the laws only apply to public water sources. Those who get their water from America's more than 11 million private wells must fend for themselves.

Can you do anything to guarantee the quality of your drinking water? Fortunately, yes. Many home water treatment devices that have proven to be effective removers of a wide range of contaminants are now available. Descriptions of the most common types follow.

Distillers

Today's state-of-the-art home distillers are based on ancient technology but use new materials and designs for modern effectiveness and convenience. Both air-cooled and water-cooled units are available at prices ranging from $200 to more than $700. All models use electricity and produce as much heat as a small room heater—not a particularly welcome feature in summer if the distiller is in your kitchen. Based on average electrical rates, distillers cost between 20¢ and 30¢ per gallon to operate.

Reverse-Osmosis Systems

The process of reverse osmosis (RO) was developed 35 years ago for industrial applications and the large-scale desalination of water. Now small RO systems are popular and effective home treatment devices. A system typically consists of a sediment prefilter module, a module containing an RO membrane and a carbon filter module, all of which fit neatly beneath the kitchen sink. RO systems require no electricity; they operate on the pressure of the water-supply line. A good RO system can cost anywhere between $400 and $900 to buy and costs between 5¢ and 25¢ per gallon to operate (based on the price of carbon filter replacement).

Activated Carbon Filters

The ancient Greeks filtered contaminated water through charcoal. Today, carbon filters are still one of the best devices for removing odor- and taste-causing substances, as well as chlorine and many organic contaminants. The most effective carbon filters are those that contain the most activated carbon. These units are typically mounted under the sink; some sit on the countertop. End-of-faucet units usually contain less carbon and are generally less effective than larger models. Activated carbon filters for the home cost anywhere from $10 to more than $300 and operate at a cost of 5¢ per gallon or less.

Bottled Water

An alternative to home treatment devices is bottled water. Unfortunately, it costs up to a dollar per gallon, and bottled water is not guaranteed to be much different from ordinary tap water. Some brands, in fact, *are* ordinary tap water, filtered, bottled, and hyped. The best you can do is find a brand that agrees with your palate and your pocketbook. And save plenty of room in the refrigerator.

The First Step: Diagnosing Your Drinking Water

Before spending hundreds of dollars on a home water treatment system, it's a good idea to find out whether you really need one. The only way to do that is to have your water tested.

Unfortunately, water testing can be a complicated and expensive process. More and more laboratories are gearing their services to the residential market, but it still helps to do some homework to ensure that you neither have your water overtested (expensive) nor undertested (potentially hazardous to your health).

First, are there any obvious problems with your water? Does it look brown or murky? Does it foam when you splash it around in a glass? Does it have a distinct taste or smell? Positive answers to any of these questions may indicate the presence of detergents, silt, rust, decaying organic matter, algae, chlorine, dissolved minerals, or synthetic chemicals.

Next, take note of any activities in your area that may be affecting the quality of the local water supply. Farms, landfills, industrial plants, mines, and gas stations are all potential sources of groundwater contaminants. Ask your neighbors if they've had any problems with their water, and try to get water test reports from your municipal treatment plant.

Then report your observations to a qualified water treatment professional. You can find one through your local water department, state department of health, or a lab approved by the Environmental Protection Agency. (Some are listed in the Yellow Pages under "Water Analysis.") Mail-order testing is another alternative. One well-established mail-order lab is the WaterTest Corporation (P. O. Box 186, New London, NH 03257). For under $100, they will analyze your water sample and help you interpret the results.

APPLIANCES

Major appliances are expensive, and although their primary purpose is functional, they play a big part in the "look" of a kitchen. Small appliances have a part to play in today's kitchen, too. You'll want to consider which are the smart small appliances to have and which ones are best left in the store. In this chapter we'll give you guidelines to help you make wise decisions when choosing these items. We'll consider both function and design.

Through the years we've seen a lot of *colors* come and go in kitchen appliances: yellow, pink, avocado, gold, brown, turquoise. The trend these days is toward appliances in neutral shades or ones with black-glass fronts, which make dramatic statements in both wood and laminate kitchens. White, it seems, will always be with us and maintains its popularity. Almond is another popular choice.

Now that kitchens are for more than cooking, it's important for appliances to look as if they are part of the total design of the room. *Trim kits*, used to panel refrigerators, dishwashers, and compactors so that they match cabinets or other appliances, function as camouflages. It is not unusual for a refrigerator to look more like a cabinet than a refrigerator.

If you're giving your kitchen a total makeover, you can easily spend $4,000 or more on a new range, refrigerator, dishwasher, garbage disposal, and other modern marvels such as microwave ovens, warming drawers, and barbecue units. If you're remodeling, you'll want to consider which appliances you can keep and which you must replace. If your existing appliances work well but don't match your new color scheme, you can use trim kits to panel the dishwasher, trash compactor, or refrigerator to match new cabinets. It is even possible to have a local auto-body shop repaint a refrigerator to match a new decor.

Appliances often have *electronic controls* that take the guesswork out of running them. Microwave ovens, for example, are programmed to cook exactly as you wish. Controls on dishwashers tell you how much time a cycle takes, and controls on refrigerators tell you when everything is operating normally.

You will want to consider the *energy consumption* of any new appliance you buy.

Energy-efficient appliances save you money during the lifetime of their operation, and that can be a selling point if you ever decide to sell your home.

Federal laws require that manufacturers put EnergyGuide labels on furnaces, refrigerators, refrigerator/freezers, water heaters, clothes washers, dishwashers, and room air conditioners. These yellow tags tell you the estimated yearly operating cost of an appliance, so that you can do some comparison shopping.

Kitchen ovens and ranges, microwave ovens, and televisions do not carry these tags. It is possible, though, to figure out energy consumption if you know the number of hours per year that an appliance is used and the energy consumption in kilowatts per hour. Manufacturers' representatives can tell you approximately how many kilowatt-hours their appliances consume in a year. If an appliance consumes, for example, 1,200 kilowatt-hours a year and you pay 8¢ per kilowatt-hour, it costs $0.08 \times 1,200$ or $96.00 a year to operate. If you find calculating energy costs a problem, ask the consumer services personnel at your local electric or gas utility company for assistance.

When you select appliances, both major and minor, for your new kitchen, you will have lots to consider: how they look, how they perform, and how energy efficient they are.

What's Cooking?

Do you want a freestanding range? A slide-in unit that functions like a built-in? Or a cooktop and a separate, built-in oven? And about that oven—will you stay with a conventional one, or will you choose a convection type, a microwave, or a combination of microwave and conventional heat or a combination of microwave and convection heat? These are a few of the many choices you'll have to make about how you will cook in your new kitchen. First, though, you'll have to decide whether you'll cook with gas or electricity.

Gas or Electricity

Many cooks swear by gas, but James Beard, among others, used nothing but an electric range. Traditionally, gas cooking has been more popular because of its great responsiveness; electric burners have always taken much longer to heat up and cool down. But new electric elements heat up almost instantly, and you can regulate the heat very accurately. If you can't make a

If you can't make up your mind, install a gas *and* electric cooktop.

decision between gas or electric, you can have the best of both worlds. Gaggenau USA Corporation makes a cooktop that has both gas and electric burners!

Gas cooking has been implicated as a major source of indoor air pollution in today's tighter houses. If you cook with gas, be sure to have—and to use—an effective venting system to exhaust the fumes outdoors. (See "Breathing Easier in the Kitchen" on page 62.)

Cooktops

When you select your cooktop, you will have to consider both your cooking needs and the "look" you want. For example, you might select a *convertible cooktop* with two traditional coil electric elements and with a barbecue grill that can be replaced by a griddle, a deep-fat fryer, a rotisserie, or a wok. A convertible cooktop allows you to suit your cooking needs exactly.

Indoor barbecue units are becoming very popular. Unless you have a large kitchen and therefore have room for a large cooktop, you'll probably need to get a barbecue unit that's removable and can be replaced by conventional burners when it's not in demand.

Hot news in kitchen ranges these days is induction cooking. In an *induction cooktop* a panel of glass ceramic conceals the induction coils. These coils conduct heat directly to iron or steel pans and pots, which are the kinds that must be used in induction cooktops. This type of cooktop is somewhat easier to clean than conventional cooktops because spills can't go through the cooktop.

If you are into European design in your new kitchen, you'll want to consider a *European-style cooktop*. This cooktop has cast-iron electric elements set into tempered glass. Cleanup time for these cooktops is also somewhat easier because spills can't go through the elements or the cooktop.

A separate cooktop and wall oven cost more than a single freestanding unit. But there are many advantages in separating them if your space and budget allow. With a stand-alone cooktop, you can use the space underneath for storing cookware. That's a

This convertible cooktop has four elements and a grill that can be replaced by other units (griddle, deep-fat fryer, rotisserie) to suit your cooking needs.

good place for a bank of drawers, to save opening a cupboard and then pulling out a shelf. Another advantage to an ovenless cooktop is that you won't have to stand in front of a hot oven while tending your pans and skillets. And, since you won't use the oven as often as you use the cooktop, you can give the oven a place outside of your kitchen's main work triangle.

Ranges

If you're not going to have separate appliances, a slide-in range can give you many of the advantages of a built-in unit. Its cooktop has a rim that sits on top of the counter and keeps food from spilling down the sides of the oven.

The worst thing about a freestanding range is the space that will be left between counter and cooktop. Spattered grease and spilled food will find their way into those cracks, and you'll occasionally need to move the heavy appliance out to clean its sides, the adjoining cabinets, and your floor.

Most ranges and cooktops have four burners. But if you're going with a separate cooktop, there are now two-burner units available; you can space them as you please along your counter. A range's four burners are typically arranged two by two, in a square or rectangular pattern. But now there are also staggered arrangements—with the two front burners farther apart than the back burners—and diagonal configurations, with the back burners set off from the front ones at an angle. Any of these can work, but be

sure the pattern you choose matches the way you cook.

To decide if a cooktop (either separate or on a range) will offer you the space you need, measure from the center of one burner to the center of the next one, then compare those measurements with the sizes of your favorite pots and pans. You'll need 9½ inches between burners to place two 5-quart Dutch ovens on the same side of a cooktop, and many large frying pans take even more room.

A note about European appliances: European ranges have been available for a couple of years now and include a good-looking, 24-inch cooktop with the oven under it or separate. European models tend to be

A four-oven Aga cooker has ovens for simmering, warming, roasting, and baking. The boiling plate and simmering plate on the top have insulating lids to retain heat and keep the cooker ready for immediate use.

A slide-in range is flush with the countertop. The rim sits on the countertop and prevents spills from running down the sides of the oven.

a little sleeker than American appliances, and if you're looking for an apartment-size range, a European model could be just what you need.

The cast-iron Aga cooker, which is from Great Britain and is often called the Rolls Royce of cookers because of its performance and cost, is now available in North America. In the Aga, unlike conventional ranges, most of the cooking is done in the ovens (rather than on the boiling and simmering plates), and this cooker works on the principle of heat storage. It is always on, but an insulating jacket keeps the heat in the cooker and conserves fuel. (The cooker uses gas or coal.) If you cook for a large household or for crowds, the four-oven model is an appropriate size. Otherwise, a two-oven model will do.

Ovens

Should your new kitchen include more than one oven? Two are very handy if you do a lot of baking and often need to bake at different temperatures at the same time. If you'd like an extra baking oven and you're planning on a microwave, you could get both by selecting a combination microwave-convection oven.

Microwave ovens are designed for three types of cooking: fast cooking, defrosting, and reheating. Microwave ovens come in a wide range of sizes and with a variety of features. These ovens sit on countertops, or they can be mounted underneath cabinets, built into cabinets, recessed into walls, or installed over ranges. (Some models replace a vent hood because the vent is built into the range.) To date, the doors on microwave ovens swing open from the right side only.

A commercial range is great for a restaurant, but give this option careful consideration before installing one in a home kitchen.

Amana Refrigeration makes one model with a door that opens down, which would be useful if your microwave were to be installed in a corner.

When you are selecting an oven, open it and measure the inside dimensions, since the outside size will not be a good indication of what you'll find when the door is open.

If you can find the space for it, a warming drawer is a wonderful luxury. You can use it to warm plates or rolls and to keep a meal warm while waiting for late diners or enjoying your first course. Warming drawers cost about $300 and will fit under your oven or in any other convenient space.

Commercial Ranges

In some circles, commercial ranges are all the rage. These are the very same ranges

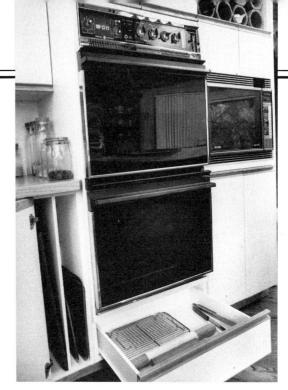

This oven center has two conventional ovens and a microwave. The pans and utensils for these ovens are stored in the center, too.

Vents are a good idea for electric ranges, because they remove moisture and cooking odors.

that are used in restaurant kitchens. They are designed to be simple and functional. There are no gadgets to be found on these ranges, and they'll last almost forever.

A commercial range offers a serious cook a much higher heat for cooking and the opportunity to cook for crowds. Such a range throws off large amounts of heat during cooking and even when it's not being used for cooking. (These ranges retain heat longer than a conventional range, and pilot lights in gas ranges keep them warm.) In both cases your kitchen can get very hot—so hot that some cooks find it nearly impossible to use these ranges in summer. The Aga cooker (see pages 59-60) is a sensible alternative to a commercial range because it gives off much less heat.

Commercial ranges must be installed properly. Be sure you have adequate ventilation and protect the surfaces around the range from the high heat it produces. Commercial ranges are heavy, too. Make sure that your floor can support one if you decide to go with this type of range.

The most popular restaurant ranges for the home are either the 36-inch size with six burners and one oven or the 60-inch size with six burners, a griddle, and a broiler over two ovens. Experts say that commer-

61

Breathing Easier in the Kitchen

Is your cooking making you sick? It's not your Chicken Cacciatore we're casting doubt on, but rather its preparation. Because if you're cooking with a gas range and don't have adequate ventilation, you could be endangering the health of your family.

When a gas flame burns, it gives off pollutants, just like every type of combustion. You wouldn't light a fireplace without first opening the flue, but that's what you're doing, on a smaller scale, when you turn on a gas range that's not vented outdoors.

You can see and smell wood smoke, but emissions from gas ranges are odorless and invisible. They include carbon monoxide, formaldehyde, sulfur dioxide, nitric oxide, and tiny particles of soot. According to one study, levels of nitrogen dioxide pollution in homes with gas ranges are often twice as high as those outdoors. And now that people are building tighter homes and buttoning up older ones, these pollutants are hanging around the house for a longer time.

Researchers still have a lot to learn about the health effects of indoor air. But in at least one study, 5- to 11-year-old children living in homes with gas ranges were found to have more colds, bronchitis, and respiratory ailments than children living in homes with electric ranges.

So what can you do about gas-range pollution? The best answer is to install a range hood that's vented outdoors or to install a cooktop that has an exhaust vent to the outdoors. Such a vent carries combustion emissions directly outside the house and can reduce range-generated pollution levels by 60 to 90 percent. Unvented, recirculating hoods with charcoal filters are a different breed. While effective for trapping grease and removing odors, they do little to combat indoor pollution. Another consideration is to buy a gas cooktop with electronic ignition. Such a cooktop doesn't have a standing pilot light, which means no pollution goes into the air until the cooktop is on.

But vented range hoods, while ideal, aren't always practical, especially if the range is against an interior wall. And maybe you aren't ready to replace your old gas cooktop with one that has an exhaust system. What then? Consider installing a compact *air-to-air heat exchanger* in your kitchen. This boxlike device, usually recessed into a wall between studs, draws fresh air into the house while exhausting stale, polluted air. Because it transfers warmth from the outgoing to the incoming air, there's very little heat loss.

One excellent kitchen-size unit is Lossnay Model VL-1500 VC, manufactured by Mitsubishi Electric Sales America. Measuring 21 by 15 inches, the Lossnay uses only 50 watts of electricity and can be installed in a window opening or in an external wall. It costs about $300.

The alternative to a range hood for a gas cooktop is a cooktop that has a down-draft vent to the outside. The vent at the back is raised when this cooktop is on, and it is flush with the cooktop when not in use.

cial ranges from different companies are roughly equal in quality, but prices for a particular brand vary considerably, depending on how far you are from the manufacturing site.

Perhaps the best choice might be to install a commercial cooktop or several commercial burners, which provide the high heat of a restaurant range but won't dramatically raise the temperature of the kitchen. Then, install a conventional oven separately.

Ventilation

While you're looking at cooking appliances, consider what kind of venting system you're going to install. As mentioned above, there are potential problems with gas appliances, and even if you're cooking on an electric range, you'll need a good exhaust system to take care of the moisture put into the air by cooking.

Any range hood you install should be at least as wide as your cooktop—a little wider if possible. Be sure to follow the manufacturer's instructions about how high to mount the hood. A hood that's too high won't do the job. And check the power of the fan; it should circulate at least 300 cubic feet per minute at its maximum speed. Something called the *sones* rating will tell you how noisy the fan will be; the higher the rating, the louder the fan. Choose a fan with a rating of 8 or less.

If it annoys you to cook with a range hood right in front of you, or if your cooktop is on an island, then a downdrafting exhaust system could be the answer. This is a relatively new venting option, but almost every manufacturer now offers it. Remember, though, that some of the space under the cooktop will have to be reserved for the system's mechanisms.

If you can't find a way to vent your kitchen's air to the outside, there are recirculating range hoods that simply draw air from your kitchen through a system of filters and then blow it back into the room. For this kind of hood to work at all, its filters must be kept very clean. And even then it won't be nearly as effective as passing the air directly to the outside.

Pots and Pans

When selecting cookware, function should be your first consideration. Your choices will reflect your cooking style. What do you require pots and pans to do? A serious cook can make good food in virtually any type of utensil but will not want to make do over the long term. Someone who cooks infrequently will not want to spend thousands of dollars on copper cookware.

Cookware is made from a number of different materials—there is no single ideal material for all pots and pans. Copper is great for sauté pans—sautéing requires a pan that is highly conductive and cools quickly. These attributes are wasted in a stockpot, though. Pots and pans for different purposes have different shapes: the low, rounded sides of an omelet pan make it easier to shape an omelet.

For this reason, serious cooks often choose pots and pans individually for the tasks they perform best. Whether you do this or not will depend on how you cook. Do you make sauces that need split-second timing or do you reheat frozen foods in the microwave? Do you cook for a large family or only a few people? Do you need special-

Certain pots and pans do their jobs well (clockwise from the top left: a copper sauteuse for sautéing, braising, and sauce making; an earthenware casserole and porcelain souffle baker that work in all ovens; a cast-iron skillet, a workhorse in the kitchen; a glass baking dish for use in all ovens; saucepans that are nonreactive transmit heat well and are easy to clean; and an oval casserole that can go from range to oven to table).

ized utensils or will a few general-purpose pots and pans suffice?

Your cookware selection will depend on your appliances. If you use a microwave, you'll need glass, porcelain, or earthenware baking dishes. (These materials do not function well on top of the range.) Some paper products also make microwave cooking fast and easy. You can only use magnetic cookware, such as cast iron or enamel-covered steel, on an induction cooktop. (If a magnet sticks to the bottom of the pot, it can be used on an induction cooktop.)

Finally, don't ignore the decorative value of cookware. Pots and pans grouped on a wall or hung from a rack make an effective, utilitarian display and are close at hand to the busy cook. An earthenware casserole

63

can add a primitive touch. Just remember that pots and pans get dirty. A display of copper pots is impressive, but polishing them takes time. Is it worth it to you?

The Big Chill

Your food-shopping habits help you decide how large a refrigerator to buy. The more often you shop, the less refrigerator space you'll need. One rule of thumb says that you should have a total of 12 cubic feet of space for the first two members of the family and 2 more cubic feet for each additional member of the household.

If you covet a built-in look for your refrigerator, Sub-Zero Freezer Company, AEG, and Gaggenau USA Corporation manufacture refrigerators shallow enough to line up with the rest of your 2-foot-deep cabinets. Traulsen & Company, long known for its commercial refrigerators, makes residential refrigerators now that resemble the commercial models. These models are 24 inches deep, so they are flush with cabinets.

All is not lost, though, if you don't have a refrigerator that is flush with the cabinet fronts. Many brands of refrigerators can have that built-in look if you use a trim kit to match them to the exterior of your cabinets. Also, major appliance manufacturers are aware of the "look" of their appliances. One refrigerator has a textured exterior that looks great and hides fingerprints. This design goes well with laminate cabinets with a textured pattern.

Whatever its size, your refrigerator will probably be put together in one of three ways: with the freezer on top, the freezer on the bottom, or the freezer and refrigerator compartments side by side. In most top-and-bottom arrangements, the freezer is on top; that tends to be the most energy-efficient configuration. But from a cook's perspective, the top is not the best place for a freezer. It's nicer to have the refrigerator section, used more frequently, up at eye level. At least three manufacturers—Amana, Whirlpool, and Sub-Zero—still offer bottom-freezer models. Side-by-side refrigerators rank last in energy efficiency, and unless you buy a very wide one, you may find it

hard to locate frozen foods inside the deep, narrow freezer compartment.

If space in your new kitchen is really at a premium, there are refrigerators available that have either a tiny freezer or none at all. And you can get under-the-counter refrigerators if windows or islands in your plan leave you without adequate wall space. There are even some tiny European refrigerators that will fit inside a standard-depth (24-inches-deep) base cabinet. These diminutive coolers are only 24 inches wide

This refrigerator is 2 feet deep and therefore flush with standard cabinets. This is the ultimate in a built-in look.

The commercial look in home refrigerators means stainless steel and glass. This particular refrigerator is also available with glass doors.

and are perfect for someone who wants a refrigerator that's out of sight and out of mind.

High-tech electronic controls are found in refrigerators, too. They monitor operation and keep you informed when things are functioning well and when they aren't. Other special features abound in refrigerators. You can select such things as ice-cream makers, ice makers, and water, juice, wine, or soda dispensers. You'll need to decide which special features you and your family really need.

Cold Storage outside the Kitchen

Under certain circumstances, you may want to install a refrigerator or a freezer

Energy-Efficient Refrigerators

When saving energy began paying off, manufacturers had an incentive to improve the efficiency of kitchen appliances. American refrigerators increased in efficiency by 59 percent from 1972 to 1981. Apparently, the Japanese did even better. A typical Japanese refrigerator is said to use 45 percent less energy per unit volume than an equivalent American refrigerator; however, they feature fewer of the conveniences Americans seem to want and are very difficult to obtain in this country.

One reason Japanese refrigerators are more energy efficient is because they are smaller; in general, the smaller the refrigerator, the more efficient. But most of the energy savings in recent models are due to advances in design, technology, and engineering—for example, more efficient compressor motors, a better foam insulation, and independent temperature control of refrigerator and freezer compartments.

The Japanese have achieved efficiency without sacrificing self-defrosting. Most manufacturers use the American-style method of automatic self-defrosting; the refrigerators defrost several times a day. A refrigerator manufactured by Toshiba America employs an innovative, manually initiated defrost. One to three times a year, when frost buildup becomes too thick, a homeowner pushes a button and the freezer compartment defrosts and then resets itself. Toshiba claims that this system offers more cooling capacity, more space in the freezer, and less noise. Apparently, Japanese consumers do not think this system is inconvenient, since Toshiba's sales are growing.

While energy-efficient appliances are generally more expensive initially, they pay back in the long run. A recent report suggested that buying these appliances is an excellent investment; the extra money spent, in most cases, typically returns 10 to 58 percent a year in operating-cost savings. This return is above inflation and is tax free!

The American Council for an Energy-Efficient Economy (ACE 3) publishes a biannual ranking of the most energy-efficient home appliances, including refrigerators. These reports cost $2 and are available from the American Council for an Energy-Efficient Economy (ACE 3), 1001 Connecticut Avenue NW, Suite 535, Washington, DC 20036.

somewhere outside your kitchen. There are several good reasons for doing this, but the most basic is to gain space.

Putting your major refrigerator or freezer elsewhere may enable you to get by with a small unit in your kitchen—perhaps an imported, efficient space-saver—for storing necessities. The auxiliary can hold bulkier, less frequently used foods.

For a *totally* built-in look, use a trim kit so the exterior of the dishwasher matches the cabinetry.

Locating a freezer outside the kitchen makes good sense. A freezer in a garage or basement will not be inconvenient if it is used for long-term storage. This may be the only solution for large families that require a refrigerator/freezer in the kitchen and need additional freezer space. For others, a small freezer in the kitchen takes care of short-term storage and necessities such as ice. Some people even prefer a refrigerator with a very small freezer and a small freezer placed outside of the kitchen.

If you're considering locating the refrigerator outside of the kitchen to save space, perhaps you could put it in a small room nearby and turn that room into a pantry.

People who entertain frequently often locate a refrigerator in the area where they entertain. A small refrigerator is a natural adjunct to a wet bar and can eliminate trips to the kitchen.

Cleaning Up

Your dishwasher may be a little easier to select than the rest of your new kitchen appliances. You basically have three different choices: an under-the-counter (built-in dishwasher), an under-the-sink model, or a portable (mobile) model with a countertop.

With the exception of one model that fits into a space 18 inches wide, built-in dishwashers are all made to a standard height and width. They're meant to fit in under a standard 36-inch counter. The exposed front of the dishwasher can match the color of other appliances, or you can use a trim kit to panel the front to match your cabinets.

If your kitchen is small and cramped for space, you'll want to consider an under-the-sink dishwasher. This model fits into a space that is often underused in a kitchen.

When you shop for a dishwasher, you will want to consider special features, such as a built-in hot-water booster. With this device, you can set the thermostat of the water heater that services your house at 110° or 120°F and still wash your dishes in hot water. The booster in the dishwasher will heat water to 140° or 150°F—the recommended dishwasher temperature. If your old dishwasher doesn't have a hot

water booster and it works well, there is still a way to conserve hot water. You can install a tankless, point-of-use water heater near the dishwasher, probably under the sink, to boost the temperature of the water used in the dishwasher up another 30°F.

Other features to consider are the dishwasher's controls, which range from simple dials to electronic controls operated by touch. You'll have to decide which of the many options are necessary for you and your family.

Garbage Disposal

Shopping for a new garbage disposal isn't a great deal of fun, since it won't be a visual part of your new kitchen. In any case, it won't take a big bite out of your budget. Even the most expensive one is only a couple hundred dollars—probably a good investment since the top-of-the-line model will come with extra horsepower, an antijam mechanism, and better insulation to reduce the noise. You can choose batch feed or continuous feed. That's just a matter of personal preference.

Small Appliances

Among the host of small appliances that vie for consumer attention and dollars are some that are so versatile or perform a certain task so well that they have become as essential in most kitchens as a range.

The food processor revolutionized cooking at home as well as in restaurants and is perhaps the most versatile small appliance. Food processors can shred vegetables, cut them into various shapes, knead dough, mix, chop meat, and perform a myriad of other tasks. Virtually the only major food preparation chore out of the reach of most food processors is whipping egg whites or cream. Cuisinarts, the largest producer of food processors in America, recently introduced an accessory that will do this.

The best food processors have built-in circuit breakers to shut off the machine before it overheats, large work bowls, and expanded feed tubes to accommodate a wide range of foods. If you are looking for a food processor, make sure it can do what you expect—that its motor is strong enough to handle the large batches of dough you want it to knead, for example. Various attachments enable food processors to grate ice, make pasta, or juice citrus fruits.

Over 90 percent of American households own an electric coffee maker. Yet despite this near universality, coffee makers continue to sell well. One reason is that the machines are constantly evolving. Coffee makers not only prepare the style of coffee one favors—percolated (the old American standard), drip, even espresso—but grind beans to order, and begin brewing at a preset time so that fresh coffee is available when desired.

Another popular coffee-making appliance is the coffee grinder. One style resembles a miniature blender; coffee is ground by its whirling blades. The coffee mill crushes coffee between small wheels, yielding a more even grind.

Heavy-duty mixers are self-contained units for countertop use. Standard attachments accomplish a variety of tasks—a whip beats egg whites and whips cream, and a dough hook kneads bread dough. With additional attachments, some mixers become food processing centers and do everything from making pasta to stuffing sausage casings. Some are electronically controlled and will not stall at low speeds, affording a great

Some small appliances are virtually essential in the well-equipped kitchen (clockwise from the top left: a food processor that is capable of handling big processing chores; a blender suitable for heavy-duty use; a mixer that, with attachments, is a food processing center; a coffee mill that offers a large capacity and a range of grating sizes; a hot-air corn popper; and a coffee maker).

amount of control. One mixer contains a heating element in the base for preparing sauces and other dishes that must be heated and stirred.

Blenders have been important kitchen appliances for decades and perform creditably as food choppers and drink makers. The newest innovation in blenders is the immersion blender. These appliances perform the functions of a blender—finely chopping small quantities of herbs or vegetables, pureeing soft fruits, mixing drinks—in any container, even a pot. Attachments allow them to function as hand-held mixers. Since they achieve a higher RPM (revolutions per minute) than conventional blenders, some can whip skim milk into a whipped topping!

Toasters and toaster ovens are closely related. A toaster toasts individual slices of bread. At least one recently introduced model has built-in microchips that ensure even toasting of subsequent slices of bread by counting the electrical pulses needed to produce toast of a certain darkness! Toaster ovens warm or toast bulky foods such as muffins or pastries. Toaster ovens are energy-savers because they can reheat foods or broil small portions of meats or fish more efficiently than a regular oven. Both toasters and toaster ovens are now being made to fit under cabinets. European-style toasters with wider slots for toasting bulkier foods are also available.

Slow cooker is the generic name for Crockpots. Related to old-time deep fryers, slow cookers cook foods slowly over a long period of time, retaining flavor, bulk, and vitamins.

Electric corn poppers are a top-selling appliance, and popcorn is still America's number one snack. The newest electric corn poppers work by using hot air, not oil. Since the resulting snack has no greasy coating, salt crystals do not stick to the popcorn, so it is low in fat and sodium.

Cordless and Rechargeable Appliances

Cordless and rechargeable are the latest buzzwords in the housewares industry. Improvements in battery technology have permitted the design of cordless, rechargeable tools that are as powerful as a similar, plug-in device, yet are easier to store and offer the user the convenience of using them anywhere, not just within a cord's length of an outlet.

Cordless, rechargeable kitchen tools and appliances are an outgrowth of a line of cordless garden and shop tools, introduced in the mid-1970s by Black & Decker (U.S.). One tool in the otherwise undistinguished line was the forerunner of the Dustbuster. Since its introduction in 1979, over 10 million Dustbusters have been sold.

The nickel-cadmium batteries that power these appliances can be quickly and fully charged simply by plugging them into a standard AC (alternating current) outlet.

In fact, many cordless tools are sold with a mounting bracket that can be hung on the wall and plugged into an outlet, so the appliances are always recharged and ready for use.

So far, cordless, rechargeable appliances include knives, portable mixers, immersion blenders, can openers, vacuums, and the like. While these appliances are convenient and easy-to-store, they are also somewhat limited in their utility. None of the larger, stationary small appliances, like blenders or food processors, is available in cordless versions as yet.

Storing Appliances

However handy small appliances are in the kitchen, they take up space, and especially in small kitchens each square inch counts. But regardless of the size of the kitchen, each cook faces the dilemma of where to put small appliances.

One obvious solution is the countertop. This is especially good for appliances that, like coffee makers, are used daily, or for appliances that are used frequently in food preparation, like mixers and food processors. Appliances stored on counters are always at hand but must be lifted or moved when cleaning the counter.

Of course, if you don't like the appearance of these appliances, you'll want to figure out how to hide them. A popular way to conceal appliances but still keep them handy is to house them in an appliance garage. An appliance garage is a cabinet usually covered by a tambour door and installed at countertop height underneath wall cabinets, leaving the front half of the counter free. They can house one or more appliance, which can be plugged into an outlet strip at the back of the garage and will slide out, ready for use.

Appliances can be concealed in the countertop. The NuTone Food Center has a power base that is installed in the countertop; various attachments, such as a food processor, juicer, and blender, fit on top of the base. The attachments can be stored in a cabinet underneath or above the power unit.

Frequently used appliances, such as

Appliance garages keep countertops neat and uncluttered.

food processors and stationary mixers, can be permanently mounted on shelves that swing up from under the counter or inside a cabinet to countertop height. They can be plugged into an outlet mounted inside the cabinet, and shelves or racks can hold disks, extra bowls, and other accessories. For best results, mount these appliances in a cabinet at least 15 inches wide to allow some working area around the appliance.

Any appliance can be stored inside cabinets on pull-out shelves and lifted to the counter when used. Another place to store small appliances is on an area that is seldom used for storage—the wall space between the counters and overhead cabinets. In fact, the electronics revolution and the constant battle to gain space in the kitchen has spawned an entire new generation of small appliances that are designed to be mounted on the wall or fastened to the underside of overhead cabinets.

Some of these modernistic space-savers are more expensive than comparable countertop models, but manufacturers are finding that consumers will pay more for higher-quality products that do what they want. Among the space-saving appliances now available are coffee makers, blenders, can openers, clock radios, even televisions. Several of the immersion blenders on the market have plates for wall mounting. In fact, the demand for these types of appliances has been so great that demand has exceeded supply for some products.

When you assess storage for your appliances, you might find that there is no reason to store them anywhere but on the countertop. Appliance designers have been more concerned about the appearance of their products—a concern fueled by the popularity of the generally well-designed European appliances. Those who cook frequently and ambitiously will appreciate the convenience of having appliances at hand when they are needed. And since some small appliances are so well-designed, they will be visual treats sitting on countertops.

69

WALLS, FLOORS, AND CEILINGS

Walls, floors, and ceilings are your house's skeleton, the framework that supports the house and carries, conceals, and protects its vulnerable systems. This structural role requires strength balanced against the need for interior access, openness, and light. Walls, floors and ceilings define spaces. They are major elements in your decorative plan. They block sound and ensure privacy. They contain fire damage. In short, when designing your kitchen, just as in designing an entire house, you must keep in mind the many roles walls, floors, and ceilings play.

The walls are particularly vital structurally. Above the foundation, walls support a house. Although it is tempting to eliminate walls in kitchen remodeling, making the space more spacious, more open, and admitting more light, you must consider the structural impact of such changes in your planning.

Walls that play a structural role are called *bearing walls*. If you are remodeling your kitchen, you must realize that changes to bearing walls must be approached with caution. You cannot remove substantial portions of a bearing wall without providing alternative support for the weight the wall carries. Adding a beam and posts may allow removal of part of the wall, but in other cases the wall may have to stay intact. Before making any changes to a bearing wall, consult a qualified engineer, architect, or builder.

Besides holding up the weight of the house, walls provide support for cabinets, shelves, racks, and fixtures. By eliminating walls, you cut down on the amount of overhead storage available, although some overhead storage systems can be suspended between posts or fastened to the ceiling.

Walls afford a permanent way to channel traffic flow, but they don't have to run from floor to ceiling. Islands and peninsulas also direct traffic, and well-placed furniture groupings—perhaps a dining table and chairs—are an effective but less permanent means of making sure traffic goes where you want it to go. Columns and posts necessary for supporting a bearing wall can also direct traffic.

Walls and ceilings are pierced to admit light through windows, doors, and skylights. If your kitchen is dark and closed in, it may be easy to remove a portion of a wall to install a window, pass-through, or door, or

you may be able to punch a hole through the roof for a skylight, opening up the interior and admitting light. Or an entire wall and part of the ceiling may become a sunspace, allowing you to bring the outdoors into your kitchen.

Finally, walls, floors, and ceilings play a large role in the decorative scheme of your kitchen. You will need to consider how they will harmonize with the other elements in your kitchen—the major furniture (cabinets, islands, and other furniture like tables and chairs)—as well as how they will complement adjacent rooms. In selecting wall and floor coverings, your concerns will encompass durability as well as ease of cleaning, an important concern in the kitchen.

Walls

Because walls take less of a beating than floors or counters, you have greater latitude in the choice of coverings for your kitchen walls. Some materials offer naturally beautiful colors and subtle, attractive textures that are very fashionable right now. Others are bright and vibrant. Just keep in mind that while wall coverings don't need to be as durable as flooring, ease of cleaning is a real virtue in the kitchen.

Walls affect the interior of a room differently, depending on the material used to cover them. Light bounced off a light-colored wall can make a room seem larger. Wood-covered walls are warmer than painted

71

walls. A wall that will be a background for objects should be "silent," its covering a solid color, wood, or a muted pattern that will not detract from artwork, utensils, furniture, or other objects displayed against the wall. If covered with a bold print or tiles laid in a graphic pattern, a wall makes a bold statement on its own terms.

Whatever wall covering you choose, remember that all surfaces in the kitchen are exposed to many different kinds of dirt. Wall covering must resist greasy dirt, as well as acids and spills of all kinds. It should be easy to clean. Unfinished wood is impractical on kitchen walls—it will be stained forever the first time someone splashes grape juice on it.

The choices of materials for kitchen wall coverings are many—ceramic tiles, masonry and masonry veneers, paint, sheet paneling with real or simulated wood or decorative faces, wallpaper, solid wood paneling, and even laminates.

While solid wood paneling can be nailed directly to the raw, wooden studs that are used for framing a wall, most wall coverings are installed on top of a surface already fastened to the studs, usually drywall (such as Sheetrock). Drywall, large sheets of gypsum covered with paper, is inexpensive, sturdy, fire resistant, and is installed quickly. Holes are covered with thin layers of plasterlike joint compound, and joints between sheets are sealed with this compound and covered with thin tape.

Ceramic tile is as beautiful and durable on walls as it is elsewhere. It is easy to clean, is noncombustible, and makes an ideal material to install behind a range. (Local fire codes may dictate a fireproof surface around your range.) Masonry and masonry veneers are fireproof, but their surfaces make them difficult to clean, even when well sealed. Laid-up stone and real brick, while beautiful and dramatic, are very heavy and must have substantial support underneath.

Wallpaper and paint are perennial favorite wall coverings. Both are relatively inexpensive (although some wallpapers are costly) and available in a huge selection of colors. Wallpapers are now available in a whole range of textures. Some are fabrics covered with vinyl.

If you choose paint as a wall covering, you'll probably use a gloss or semigloss latex enamel. These paints stand up to wear and tear and are water resistant. Painting is an ideal do-it-yourself activity. Latex paints dry quickly, and you can clean up tools and spills with soap and water.

Even wallpaper is relatively simple for a homeowner to install, since wall-covering companies have actively pursued the do-it-yourself market. This means that you can change your kitchen's appearance simply, quickly, and cheaply by repainting or repapering. Vinyl-covered wallpaper provides an easily cleaned surface. Other wallpapers and latex paints can be cleaned, although their surfaces are more delicate and should not be scrubbed.

Neither wallpapers nor paints are fire resistant. Neither will cover flaws in a wall surface. Drywall must be carefully sealed with joint compound and plaster patched before painting or papering.

Sheet paneling is sold in a variety of surfaces and finishes, from a close approximation of real barn siding (with a baked-on vinyl finish) on a sheet of plywood, to wood grain photographically produced on hardboard, to decorator panels with designs or murals painted on them. Some paneling is structural and can be nailed directly to studs. Other kinds are thin and must be applied over drywall; it's not necessary to seal the joints of the drywall. Matching moldings cover joints. Manufacturers encourage do-it-yourselfers with clear, concise instructions for their products.

Using solid wood for paneling, whether simple pine or oak planks or more elaborately milled boards, is often expensive, but affords a range of tones and textures and a flexibility in installation unmatched by 4-by-8-foot sheet paneling. It is generally available unfinished only, which gives you great flexibility—you can stain it or bleach it. However, finishing wood is time-consuming, and the need for an easily cleaned, durable finish practically dictates using polyurethane.

Finally, you may want to consider using a plastic laminate as a wall covering. Laminates are most commonly used for backsplashes or to cover the walls above the counters and below the cabinets. They are waterproof and easy to clean. When installed vertically, a laminate is less vulnerable to scorching or scratching. Laminates harmonize particularly well with contemporary designs and European-style cabinets.

Floors

There are really only five practical choices for kitchen floors: wood, tile, brick or stone, vinyl or rubber sheets or tiles, and carpeting.

Before the development of polyurethane finishes, having wooden kitchen floors was unthinkable, but now upkeep is fairly simple. Wood is naturally beautiful and is easier on feet and legs than tile or stone. The big drawback is that wooden floors are very susceptible to water damage. Infrequent minor spills are not the problem; but in areas where continued exposure to water does occur—such as around the sink or dishwasher—the floor may warp and buckle.

Oak, which is strong, abundant, and

Wallpaper is available in many styles, textures, and colors. Here, light-colored wallpaper and curtainless windows greatly improved a once dark kitchen.

Wall Coverings

Material	Advantages	Disadvantages	Care
Ceramic tile	Wide selection of colors makes possible many imaginative designs; styles fit into any decorating scheme; noncombustible; ideal material to install around ranges and cooktops; spatters and grease clean off easily; grout resists stains and grease if well-sealed; can be installed by careful homeowner	Hard to drill if installing appliances, shelves, or other objects on walls after tiles have been hung	Clean with water and all-purpose household cleaner; scrub grout with small brush; wipe off after cleaning; steel-wool pads will scratch some tile; some tile can be cleaned with a nylon pad; check manufacturer's product claims before cleaning
Masonry and masonry veneers	Noncombustible; durable; natural colors; fascinating and varied textures; masonry veneers are light and easy for homeowner to install	Must be sealed; not easy to clean, even if sealed; not grease- or spatter-resistant; laid-up masonry walls are heavy and require extra support; difficult to drill for mounting fixtures, shelves, artwork, or other objects	Wipe with household detergent diluted in warm water; seal masonry for easiest cleaning
Paint (gloss or semigloss latex enamel best for kitchens)	Available in a huge variety of colors; tough and water-resistant; resists abrasion and smudges; can be applied by homeowner with few skills; tools and spills clean up with soap and water; can change color frequently at little expense or inconvenience	Will not hide flaws in wall surfaces—walls must be carefully cleaned and prepped before application; not fireproof	Wipe with household detergent diluted in warm water; follow manufacturer's care instructions
Sheet paneling (wood, hardboard, melamine)	Available in a variety of styles and textures and in a price range from very inexpensive to extremely	Many people find sheet paneling aesthetically unappealing; spaces between	Cleans easily—wipe with damp cloth or follow instructions provided with specific paneling

NOTE: For information on the advantages, disadvantages, and care of plastic laminates, which can be used for wall coverings, see page 49.

durable, is usually the hardwood floor of choice, although maple is sometimes used. (Maple is common in gymnasium floors.) Hardwoods hold finishes well. You can mix and match woods for decorative effects—highlighting an oak floor with a mahogany inlay—or use different styles of wooden floors, such as parquet (which has an urban feel) or countrified random-width planks.

Pine and other softwoods are, as the name implies, soft and porous. Finishes tend to wear off easily, especially in heavily trafficked areas, and it's easy to chip and dent softwood floors. But the colors of fir and pine are wonderful, and if you don't mind an annual refinishing, even a softwood floor can work.

You can cut the cost of wooden floors by installing them yourself. Lay the floor before installing the cabinets or build up the floor under the cabinets with plywood, saving the cost of more expensive flooring materials and maintaining the toe-kick space.

Floors made from ceramic tile are dura-

Material	Advantages	Disadvantages	Care
Sheet paneling (*continued*)	costly; wood paneling available in exotic, furniture-grade hardwoods at much lower cost than real woods; durable, easy-to-clean finishes; easy for homeowner to install; will mask damaged walls	some types of panels must be covered with battens, which many people find objectionable; some sheets contain urea-formaldehyde resins, which outgas	you purchase
Solid wood paneling	Beautiful, warm tones and textures; has traditional or contemporary look, depending on how it is applied and finished; since it is unfinished, you can get just the result you want; easy to install; masks damaged walls; variety of stains and surface treatments afford broad spectrum of shades	Limited choice of woods—domestic and exotic hardwoods are difficult to locate and very expensive; finishing is time-consuming and exacting; does not clean up well unless finished with smooth, hard finish like polyurethane; some wood finishes require frequent renewal and are not stain- or grease-resistant	Clean paneling that has been painted or finished with polyurethane by wiping with a soft cloth; use a nylon pad to remove stubborn stains—never a steel-wool pad or other harsh abrasives
Wallpaper	Many styles, textures, and colors to choose from; some wallpapers coordinate with fabrics and decorative accessories; vinyl-coated wallpaper is easy to clean; modern wallpapers are strippable—which means that they come off easily if you want to remove them	Hanging wallpaper is time-consuming and exacting; walls underneath must be in good condition	Wash vinyl-coated wallpaper with a sponge or a soft-bristle brush; clean stubborn spots by diluting with a small amount of bleach in clear water

ble and beautiful but are also cold and noisy. Ceramic tile is hard on feet and legs, and anything dropped on tile is guaranteed to shatter. Dark tile laid over a concrete slab is an excellent heat sink if part of your kitchen gets direct sunlight.

Tile is available in a range of stunning colors and can be worked up into an enormous number of designs. It will last forever and needs minimal care. If you decide to use a tile floor, make sure that the tiles you choose are meant for flooring and can take the amount of traffic the floor will get. Grout is now available in several colors besides the traditional white. Keeping the grout between the tiles clean is not the problem it once was, since there are a number of excellent grout sealers available.

Having tile installed can be expensive, but it is possible to do it yourself. Many tile stores encourage do-it-yourselfers by renting tools and providing clear instructions.

As flooring materials, stone and brick share the disadvantages of tile. They are

75

on the effect you wish to achieve. Old bricks, while beautiful, are extremely absorbent and very soft. If you want the appearance of old brick, select a new brick with an antique appearance.

Sheet vinyl comes in rolls 6 to 12 feet wide. There are literally thousands of patterns available, and manufacturers have developed some startlingly contemporary colors and patterns. Both sheet and tile vinyl flooring is available with a textured surface, and many designs have some surface relief.

Vinyl flooring is durable and spills clean up easily. But vinyl floors with textured surfaces will need occasional special attention to keep dirt and grime from building up around the edges. Sheet vinyl should be laid on a smooth surface, since imperfections will show. That means that some sort of underlayment must be installed first. Installing sheet vinyl is not an easy project for the do-it-yourselfer.

If you want to lay your own floor, try vinyl, cork, wood, or rubber tiles. The selection isn't as great, but the 9- to 12-inch squares are easy to lay. Some companies manufacture tiles with a layer of clear vinyl on top of a layer of cork or wood, giving the appearance of wood but making the tile virtually impervious. Rubber tiles are sometimes used in commercial kitchens because they have textured surfaces, making for surer footing on a wet floor, although the uneven surfaces are harder to clean.

Carpeting is fine to use on kitchen floors if it is vacuumed frequently and a good soil retardant sprayed on the carpeting around the range, sink, and in other areas prone to spills. Carpeted floors are easy on the feet and are shock absorbent, so that dinnerware dropped on them may not break. They are warm, a real advantage if there are small children in the house, or if your house is located in a cold climate.

While carpet is less durable than ceramic tile, it is long lasting. Some carpet is relatively inexpensive. It can be installed as a do-it-yourself project. If laid over a good pad, carpeting does much to mask flaws in the surface that it covers.

One final option you might want to consider is mixing flooring materials—for

Floor coverings should harmonize with cabinets, walls, and ceilings.

also long-wearing and offer a range of beautiful, naturally subdued colors. They can also serve as heat sinks. Stone floors are extremely heavy—even if you use thin pavers (another name for flooring tiles). If you're not installing a stone floor over a slab, make sure your floor framing will support the additional weight.

Thin brick pavers are available for use as flooring and can be installed with or without a visible mortar joint, depending example, you might want to use tiles around the sink and dishwasher but wood elsewhere. Or inset rubber tiles at stations where you will spend time on your feet.

Ceilings

Most people don't pay much attention to ceilings. This is not surprising. Although ceilings take up as much square footage as floors, they are seldom as interesting. It is almost as if the ceiling treatment is an afterthought. While ceilings are less important structurally than walls or floors, they can play a big role in the kitchen as a base for hanging lights and affixing storage systems and other fixtures, including kitchen cabinets. Because many of these function as decorative elements, ceiling treatments need to be silent—solid colors, woods (either solid woods or sheet paneling), and, more rarely, paper of one kind or another. Tiles and masonry are too heavy for extensive use on ceilings.

Ease of cleaning is as important in choosing a covering for the ceiling as it is in choosing wall coverings. While kitchen ceilings receive much less abuse than floors or walls, they are still exposed to greasy, smoky dirt. Ceilings over a range may also be subject to cooking accidents—more than one cook has washed off the ceiling when canning.

The ceiling finish affects lighting design. A light-colored, glossy ceiling reflects light. A wood-covered or dark-colored ceiling absorbs light.

If noise is a problem, covering the ceiling with acoustical tile will help modulate airborne sound, which would otherwise bounce off hard ceiling and wall surfaces. Unfortunately, many people find acoustical tile aesthetically objectionable.

Ceilings can be made more striking in a number of ways. A skylight adds light to the room and interest to the ceiling. Decorative borders, which can be stenciled on a painted wall or purchased by the roll and pasted to the wall, add interest to the ceiling. A crown molding made of several kinds of stock moldings may encircle the room, drawing attention to the ceiling. A ceiling may be

textured by using a textured paint, plaster over drywall, or a textured paneling or wallpaper. The plane of the ceiling may be broken by beams—either wooden or artificial wood or laminate covered.

A once-popular ceiling that is even more popular after its recent revival is the pressed metal ceiling, usually made of sheet steel or copper. A metal ceiling provides a real period touch—with the added benefits of being lightweight and fireproof.

Windows

We've come a long way from the days when having a window in the kitchen meant covering a hole over the sink with greased paper. There are many exciting options open to today's homeowner. You can pick a window from among five different styles: awning windows, sliders, double-hungs, casements, fixed pane. If a window can't be placed in the wall, drop a skylight (either fixed or operable) into the roof. You may achieve the effect of a window with a French door or a sliding door. Part of a wall, an entire wall, or most of a room can be glass.

Areas of glass can enhance a kitchen architecturally and decoratively. But if their only function is to admit light, that would be reason enough to install as many windows as possible. Daylight is not only the best work light but provides excellent color rendering. And it's free. Besides, as professionals who design offices are just beginning to learn, people prefer natural light.

Windows or areas of glass are particular assets in a small kitchen. They can open the kitchen up, providing a feeling of spaciousness even if the room does not grow by a single square inch. In effect, the area on the other side of the glass becomes part of the kitchen. The effect becomes reality if, instead of a window, one uses a glass door; the other room becomes an extension of the kitchen—when you want it to be. A wall may be bumped out with a bay window, providing a cozy nook for dining or extra counter space.

In what would otherwise be solid walls, windows and doors allow appreciation of or even participation in the outdoors from

Floor Coverings

Material	Advantages	Disadvantages	Care
Carpeting	Easy on the feet and legs; shock-absorbent; warm and soft—particularly good for small children; masks flaws in under-layment	Limited range of color choices and designs; spills don't clean up as easily as with other materials	Vacuum several times weekly to remove soil; spray carpeting around stove and in areas prone to spillage with soil retardant; professionally clean carpeting once a year
Ceramic tile	Many beautiful colors available; offers many design options; extremely hard and durable; minimal care; can be installed by careful homeowner	Cold and noisy; unforgiving surface—breakables shatter when dropped on tile; hard on feet and legs	Spills wipe up easily; clean with water and all-purpose household cleaner; scrub grout with small brush; sponge dry with sponge mop after cleaning; steel-wool pads will scratch some tile; some tile can be cleaned with a nylon pad; never wax glazed tile; check manufacturer's product claims before cleaning
Resilient tiles (vinyl, rubber, cork)	Easy for homeowner to install; resilient; deaden sound; cork and rubber resist dents well; rubber is waterproof	Cork stains badly unless vinyl-coated; rubber does not resist grease and requires frequent polishing to maintain gloss; all are slippery when wet, unless they have a textured sur-face finish	Vinyl and vinyl-covered tiles are durable; clean with household de-tergent; rinse clean; wax infrequently, as needed, to maintain gloss; use a nylon pad to clean stubborn spills; never a steel-wool pad
Stone (bluestone, granite, marble, slate) or brick	Extremely hard and durable; interesting colors and textures	Very heavy—floor may have to be shored up to support weight; cold and noisy; hard on feet and legs; break-ables shatter when dropped on stone or brick; stone floors with smooth finishes are slippery when wet;	Seal floors well (special sealers provide extra protection against oils and fats); cleaning up is easy —damp mop to clean up spills; floors require periodic waxing and resealing

inside the house, visually uniting interior and exterior spaces. A window may reveal a particularly spectacular view, an outdoor garden or woods, pastures, and fields. Again, a door may make this union real, opening onto a very private deck or a large space for outdoor entertaining.

Besides their architectural roles, win-dows can figure prominently in heating and ventilating plans. They admit fresh air for natural ventilation and circulation. De-pending on their orientation, windows may provide heat gain, thereby warming the indoors. Newly developed films for glass both absorb solar radiation and reflect heat back into the interior of the house so it is not lost to the outdoors.

If your intent is to gain some heat and have access to an unusual and exciting indoor space, sunspaces are particularly attractive. Under the right conditions, they can be multipurpose, functional, and deco-rative additions to a kitchen, and also help to heat the house. Sunspaces are green-

Material	Advantages	Disadvantages	Care
Stone (*continued*)		marble stains easily and shows grease and acid stains; marble scratches and nicks easily (marble in lighter colors shows fewer scratches)	
Vinyl sheets	Durable; easy on feet and legs; spills clean up easily; deaden sound	Not easy for homeowner to install; must be installed on a smooth surface; will show irregularities of under-layment; designs with textures or irregular surfaces collect dirt and must be carefully cleaned; easily dented; not resistant to burns	Many vinyls made with "No-Wax" finish; sweep vinyl No-Wax floors and clean with general-purpose liquid detergent and water; if high gloss desired, polish these floors; for Solarian (brand name) sweep floors and clean with general-purpose liquid detergent and water; shine is integral to Solarian floor and should be very long lasting; use nylon pad to clean up stubborn dirt; never use a steel-wool pad or other abrasives
Wood	Beautiful, with warm appearance; if finished with polyurethane, wood is durable and easy to clean; shock-absorbent and easy on feet and legs; homeowner can install	Softwoods dent and nick easily; must be finished with polyurethane (some wood tiles are covered with vinyl and should not be varnished; the vinyl coat affords great protection); very susceptible to water damage—continuous leaks may cause floor to buckle	Spills wipe up easily; damp mop with cold water or with EnDust or a similar product; floors made of softwoods (firs, pines) need to be refinished at regular intervals; floors finished with polyurethane are susceptible to scratches—chair legs should be padded with plastic casters or heavy-duty felt

houses meant for living. A sunspace could be used as a dining room, in which diners are surrounded by plants. If there's no room for a full-fledged sunspace, a greenhouse window can provide some heat gain and is a convenient place to grow fresh culinary herbs. Don't expect a greenhouse window to admit much light, however, since much of its space will be taken up by plants.

Windows can be decorative and attention-getting objects by themselves, no matter what's on the other side. Many com-panies make unusually shaped windows—arched, circular, hexagonal, octagonal—or sell components that can be used to build a window with a nontraditional shape. Some of these windows are fixed, others open. The glass itself doesn't even have to be clear—it can be etched, leaded, or sand-blasted, depending on the effect and type of performance desired. An artistic stained-glass panel admits light and is also visually arresting.

GALLERY
A TOUR OF FINE KITCHENS

A LIVING-HALL KITCHEN

The Tannehills' home is contemporary but echoes the tradition of New England farmhouses.

Jeremiah Eck's interest in designing living halls began when numerous clients came to him with the same request: Replace the tiny, single-use rooms in a suburban tract home with one large, multi-function room that could be the center and heart of the house. (Eck calls this quadruple-bypass heart surgery for a house.)

So when more recent clients, Judy and Terry Tannehill, asked him to design a new home, he had lots of experience with this concept. The Tannehills wanted to build a house that was contemporary but one that echoed the tradition of a New England farmhouse. Both parties, the architect and the clients, felt a distinctive need for both old and new. The result of this collaboration is a living-hall kitchen that is the heart

of the Tannehills' house. It's truly a new version of the hearth.

Judy and Terry run Whitney's Village Inn in Jackson Village, New Hampshire, and their home sits on a piece of land nearby. The mountains are literally 100 yards from their house, and floor-to-ceiling windows allow them to relish spectacular mountain views. In this house, children and adults have separate spaces, and the living hall and kitchen is the center of it all. Eck likens the house to a pinwheel in the way it uses space, with the house spinning around the kitchen and all paths leading through it.

One of the features of the kitchen the family likes best is its openness—it is open to the living hall and its magnificent stone hearth and to the greenhouse and spectacular mountain views. Someone in the kitchen is a part of everything that's going on

This living hall, with its magnificent hearth, is truly the heart of the Tannehill home.

The kitchen is open to the living hall and functions as an integral part of it. Someone working there can be a part of what's happening elsewhere in the room.

in those rooms. This is a real advantage for the Tannehills, Terry says, because they entertain a great deal. Both he and Judy cook, too, and find the kitchen a convenient workspace.

If the house spins off from the kitchen, the kitchen revolves around the central island. Its expansive butcher-block top is chopping block and chief food preparation area. The sink, set into a counter opposite, allows someone to wash foods in the sink and place them on the island. Food prepared on the island is easily moved to the grill, microwave, or range on the wall opposite the sink. Their positioning makes it easy for one person to work with all three appliances.

Meals are taken at the island, on the adjacent porch, or in the dining area, depending on how many people are dining. The counter space between the kitchen and living hall makes a handy serving area for parties. The end of the island is a convenient serving area to the greenhouse.

The cabinets feature a lazy Susan and slide-out shelves. The family particularly appreciates the appliance garages.

This is another kitchen that works well because its owners were very interested in making it work and spent the time neces-

sary to communicate their needs to a sympathetic architect. Jeremiah Eck describes the Tannehills as a contemporary couple who are nevertheless anchored in tradition—just like their modern farmhouse with the living-hall kitchen at its heart.

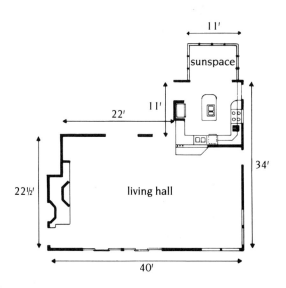

A Kitchen of Color

Colorful laminate cabinetry in the European style is the outstanding feature in this kitchen.

To some people, function is the most important consideration in designing a kitchen. To Linda Lesser, a kitchen is a kitchen. In renovating her 65-year-old ranch house, she knew that having a good workspace in the kitchen was necessary. But that wasn't where she started in planning her kitchen. For her, color was most important: "I wanted something different from white or almond,

something soothing I wouldn't get sick of," she says. What she got is a kitchen with cabinets and countertops in a unique Formica color, Fiesta Bisque. Linda worked with architect Heidi Kleinman to transform the house into a striking contemporary space, a theme strongly reflected in the kitchen. The kitchen is integrated with the rest of the Lesser house, because the colors used in the kitchen were picked up throughout, accented by harmonizing shades of light gray, lavender, and light blue. Curves in the kitchen echo curves on the outside of the house.

Furthermore, the kitchen designer created an efficient workspace that is a welcoming room for guests. Linda and Howard Lesser entertain frequently, so the kitchen contains a spacious bar with a sink, plenty of storage for glassware, and a wine rack. Since it is located out of the kitchen proper, guests can collect there without interfering with someone working in the kitchen.

The cabinets in the Lesser kitchen are custom-made. Linda did not want many built-in storage features in her cabinets. She believes they collect dirt in hard-to-reach corners—and she prefers to spend her money on what she sees. She also likes a nice, clean look in her kitchen and does not like to have appliances or cooking gear sitting on her counter. The floor-to-ceiling cabinet next to the ovens is designed so that everything is visible and easy to reach when the doors are open—a sort of closed-up open storage.

The Thermador cooktop, installed in the island, is an interesting feature. It is vented through the floor to the outside of the house. The vent on the cooktop pops up when in use. When it is not being used, its top is flush with the counter.

Lighting is another important consideration for Linda Lesser. The kitchen is lighted by recessed floodlights and by track lights. The windows over the sink admit natural light and allow Linda to look outside onto the landscaped yard and trees beyond it. Light enters the kitchen from other rooms, as well, and from windows in the outside wall above and behind the refrigerator.

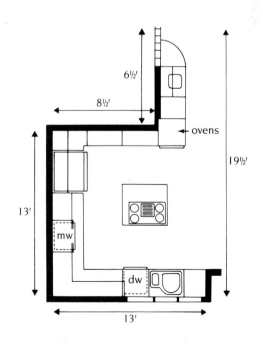

A raised ceiling with spectacular windows on the wall above the refrigerator allows light to flood this contemporary kitchen.

A Team Approach to Kitchen Design

Christie and Francis Jenkins liked their home, a sprawling colonial built in 1810, except for the 10-by-14-foot kitchen, which they had remodeled six months after buying the house. Christie cooked in that kitchen for 12 years and knew its flaws. It was too small, and there wasn't enough space for the Jenkins's three children and assorted friends to gather.

When they decided to redo their kitchen, they engaged Janine J. Newlin, CKD, ISID. The original plan was to make the old kitchen and dining area more efficient. The family decided instead to expand the kitchen. By

The look of this Jenkins kitchen is pure elegance. By expanding the original kitchen, they created space for more formal dining and for friends to gather.

The pattern of the ceramic tile planter on the island matches that of the range hood.

appliances. The cabinets were designed by Lee Kowalski, CKD, for his own Heritage cabinets showroom. Kowalski arranged for the Heritage factory to hand-stain the cabinets and finish them with a flat varnish. Matching panels conceal the Sub-Zero refrigerator and freezer, and a molding with a double bead covers the edges of the counters, further softening the kitchen's lines.

Christie Jenkins and ceramic designer Phyllis Traynor conceived the eye-catching design on the large planter and hood, and Phyllis Traynor executed it. Phyllis has perfected a technique of overglazing tiles and then firing them a second time. Janine, who conceived the process, specified American Olean tile because the company offers a variety of edge treatments that makes installation easier. The complicated planter took almost as long to design as the kitchen; it had to be well-planned to avoid excessive tile cuts.

While Janine recommended the other professionals who were engaged in the project and served as design consultant throughout the work, the Jenkins family contracted separately with everyone, and Christie Jenkins was involved in every phase of the project. As a result, the family got just what it wanted. "I can't find a flaw in this kitchen," Christie Jenkins says.

adding on, they would not just gain more space: They would also be able to see a pond that is not visible from other rooms.

A big problem initially was finding an architect who could not only design the architectural gem the family wanted but also integrate it into the house. "I wanted the extension to maintain and enhance the integrity of the original architecture," Christie Jenkins says. Architect John Eide worked up a plan that unified the addition with the older part of the house. Windows on both walls at the corner of the room give diners a new outlook on the pond. He, Janine, and Christie worked together to fit the kitchen she wanted into the addition.

All along, the family intended to install the latest Thermador appliances, but wanted to retain a country feel in the kitchen to keep it in character with the rest of the house. The warm and quietly elegant cabinetry, which features flat doors and drawer fronts with a beaded edge detail on the frames, softens the stark, contemporary

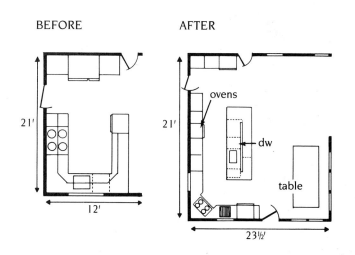

BEFORE   AFTER

A European Country Kitchen

It would be easy to imagine that Dr. and Mrs. John Cavallo's kitchen is in a farmhouse overlooking the Po River in northern Italy. Their kitchen reflects a decidedly European outlook on what makes the good country life: a generous measure of hospitality and good food shared with an extended family and friends. It also reflects their natural approach to life and good health.

Shirley Cavallo claims that her kitchen wasn't planned. She told her husband that she wanted to build a kitchen around their large, rectangular dining table—and the rest of the space evolved. But despite her disclaimer, this is a very practical kitchen, built for a no-nonsense, semiprofessional cook. For example, the distance between counters is 36 inches, so Shirley can turn and set something on the counter behind the stove without walking. There is a separate sink for cleaning vegetables, located a turn away from the refrigerator. The surfaces are easy to clean: "Ideally, I'd like to have a kitchen I could hose down," Shirley says. She has installed a four-burner range and broiler and grill, a deep sink, and some counter space right outside the kitchen door for particularly messy jobs. The Cavallos can tomatoes, peaches, and vegetables outside the kitchen since it's easier to clean and it's cooler, too. They also press grapes for wine outside.

Practicality is storing things where they will be used—linen in deep drawers adjacent to the table, for example—and in places where they are handy. Pots hang from the ceiling, appliances sit on the countertops, knives are stuck in a knife block—all close at hand for the busy cook. The commercial-weight pots and pans are both functional and a pleasure to work with.

This huge kitchen is the center of the Cavallo household, and it's constantly in use. If Shirley is not canning some of the produce from the garden or farm, she is cooking dinner for family and friends, all of whom seem to end up in the kitchen. From her work area behind the L-shaped island, Shirley can talk with her guests—or press them into service.

Despite its size, it is a warm and cozy room. "I like the warmth of wood and natural materials," Shirley says. The handmade cabinets are wooden, and the ceiling is supported by large wooden beams, in character with the rest of the seventeenth-century farmhouse. The floor is tiled in marble. Counters are butcher block (except around

The Cavallos are always prepared for feasts for 12 to 20 people. In fact, they've had up to 100 people in their home, and they ended up in the warm and inviting kitchen.

Although the Cavallo kitchen is huge, the workspace behind the L-shaped island is compact for maximum cooking convenience.

the sink) or marble slabs. Tile, which Shirley finds charming but impractical, is used only around the range and fireplace. The 5-foot Garland range was the focus of their last kitchen, which was one-sixth the size of this one.

The Cavallo kitchen is augmented by a *cantina*—a food storage room sunk into a hillside adjacent to the kitchen. It is root cellar, wine cellar, and pantry; its temperature-controlled environment allows the Cavallos to get by with a relatively small refrigerator in the kitchen and ensures that they can live the good life of Italy in the new world.

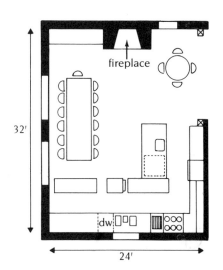

fireplace

32'

24'

dw

A Kitchen for Natural Foods Gourmets

Nikki and David Goldbeck describe themselves as "food ecologists," whose work is to help people to use traditional foods in a modern setting. The Goldbecks, authors of several natural-foods cookbooks, center their lives and their livelihoods in the kitchen.

Until recently, the Goldbecks prospered in spite of their kitchen, a cramped, 7-by-11-foot room, lighted only by a small window over the sink. But by removing a wall, the Goldbecks were able to take advantage of space in a seldom-used parlor to create a kitchen project intended to demonstrate "user friendly" kitchen design.

Foremost among the Goldbecks' priorities was convenience. Their new kitchen is packed with handy innovations for people who enjoy cooking. For example, most kitchens have only one sink; the Goldbecks' has two: one strictly for food preparation, the other for cleaning up. "A second sink makes it much easier for two cooks to work together," explains David. "It's also more hygienic to clean food in a sink separate from the one where you wash dirty dishes."

The Goldbecks' fresh approach is also apparent in their choice and utilization of cooking equipment. Like many experienced cooks, the Goldbecks prefer to cook on a gas cooktop and to bake in an electric oven. Since there's no such dual-option range on the market, the Goldbecks designed their own. Its stainless steel frame houses an electric oven and a gas cooktop, as well as drawers, shelves, and slots to store pots, pans, and utensils.

Often tall and short cooks share the same kitchen, and a counter that adapts to the person and to the task at hand is a definite convenience. At the touch of a button, one counter in the Goldbecks' kitchen lowers to desk height (27 inches) from 41 inches, or 5 inches above the standard height. To ensure reliable operation, the system rides on industrial bearings and shafts and uses a commercial-grade electric motor.

Another Goldbeck invention is a cabinet that contains movable shelves and racks and an electric heater with a blower. The Goldbecks use the cabinet as a drying rack for washed dishes or for dehydrating food, incubating yogurt, or proofing bread.

In the Goldbeck kitchen, a restored art-deco-style backsplash is the perfect mate for a new stainless steel sink. The numbers on the sandblasted glass cabinet doors function to identify what's inside.

Since there's no such appliance as a dual-option range with a gas cooktop and an electric oven, the Goldbecks designed their own. They included storage space for pots, pans, and utensils.

Like any gourmet, Nikki and David prefer fresh produce over frozen or canned. In the kitchen, herbs and greens grow in abundance on Plexiglas shelves under a newly installed skylight. A sliding sprout tray that tucks in under one of the sinks ensures a steady supply of sprouts. The Goldbecks' own special version of a root cellar—a metal box hidden away in the naturally cool crawlspace beneath the kitchen floor—preserves root vegetables and other staples of the natural foods cook. (The "cellar" is accessible via a trapdoor.)

Cleaning up is a breeze in this kitchen. A chair fits under a specially designed sink so that foot-sore dishwashers can tackle the chore in comfort. To hold food scraps for composting, the Goldbecks simply slide back a small countertop lid and drop the garbage in a plastic pail that is sealed off—odors and all—from the kitchen. The Goldbecks remove the pail from outside the house for easy dumping in their compost bin. An area to the right of the sink makes recycling cans and bottles practically effortless. The kitchen also includes energy-efficient appliances, safety equipment, ground fault interrupters to prevent electrical shock, a computer, and a special air cleaner to remove gas fumes.

Any good cook knows that food—no matter how carefully prepared—always tastes better if eaten in a room that has a special ambience. The Goldbecks are no exception; they decorated their kitchen and its adjacent dining nook with scavenged "treasures," such as a classic diner booth and "museum" of old food packages of products once wholesome but now processed.

In the Goldbeck kitchen performance is clearly first-rate. Practicality plus a distinctive style add up to money well spent.

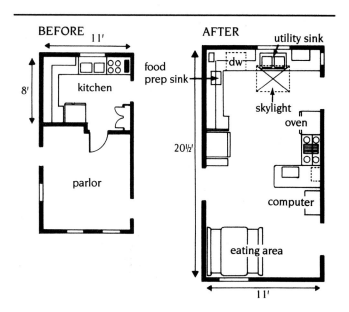

A Kitchen Created by an Aesthetect

Some people dream about a new kitchen for years and spend months planning it. Not John Calella. He decided one day to remodel his kitchen, and soon he and Bruce Sexauer, who calls himself an aesthetect (a word he coined by combining "aesthetic" with "architect"), had ripped out the old kitchen and begun the new one. Sexauer is an artist who works in wood, and this kitchen, he says, was his first serious commission. (He was a guitar maker before he began work on the Calella house.)

The kitchen is particularly important to John Calella. As "Organic John," he appears on a television series about healthful food. He teaches cooking classes and, for seven years, has hosted a call-in radio show about food and nutrition. He has three books about food and health to his credit.

When John decided to remodel the kitchen of his house, he was tackling the

The bright red sink is the perfect foil for the rich red tones of the exotic hardwoods in this kitchen.

When John Calella uses the words *beautiful* and *round* to describe his kitchen, he's right on target.

There are lots of curves in the Calella kitchen—curved molding, rounded counters, rounded cabinets, rounded windows.

room for the third time. This time, the kitchen took shape organically, as if it were naturally flowing into place. John did the basic layout of the kitchen: "I told Bruce: this is what I *feel*, this is what I *want*." Bruce says, "John tends to gesticulate and use the words 'beautiful' and 'round' a lot." He executed the kitchen design from verbal descriptions.

The Calella kitchen abounds in curvilinear forms—curved molding, rounded counters, rounded cabinets. The curves evoke natural forms and movement. They allow John to bring the feeling of nature into his house.

John chose the exotic hardwoods in the kitchen for their soft red tones. The cabinets are made of purple heart and padauk (the doors), redwood, and cedar. The floor is Italian terra-cotta tile.

Despite its rococo appearance, the kitchen is an efficient workspace. John cooks on a Wolf restaurant range—which he refers to as "the Stradivarius of stoves"—because it offers maximum control. There is a faucet and small sink next to the stove, making it easy for John to fill or rinse a pot as he works. The main sink is in the opposite corner from the stove. There is an old refrigerator in the kitchen, but no freezer because John does not cook with frozen foods.

Cutting boards of purple heart are inlaid in the tile counters. There is no dishwasher because John washes dishes by hand.

At 12 by 13 feet, the workspace is small enough that every tool is within easy reach. Light for the workspace comes from a sculpture set into the ceiling—an angel that Bruce carved has lights mounted in its wings and belly.

This organic kitchen, rich in baroque details, fits perfectly into John's health-conscious, California life-style in which good food plays a big role.

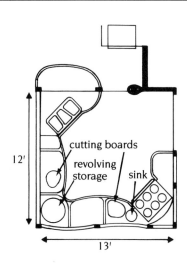

Opening Up the Galley

Diana and Richard Heinemeyer's kitchen, like their whole house, is a triumph over the constraints of small spaces. Richard, an architect, designed their compact solar home to fit on a long, narrow lot in Denver. The kitchen fits the same description: long, narrow, efficient, and bright as a sunny summer's day.

The Heinemeyers' galley kitchen fits as naturally into their lives as it fits into their floor plan. With two careers, no children, and a penchant for entertaining, they wanted a no-nonsense place for food preparation. The kitchen's modest dimensions (14 feet 8 inches by 7 feet 8 inches, with 3 feet 8 inches of floor space between the cabinets) allow for generously proportioned living and dining areas—a conscious compromise that emphasized the home's public spaces over its more intimate and utilitarian kitchen.

Yet the kitchen is neither cramped nor dreary. "Even though it's small, it doesn't feel claustrophobic," says Richard. A clerestory window brings in plenty of natural light in the daytime, collects solar warmth in winter, and creates a sense of airiness overhead. To make the hall-shaped area feel even more spacious, both ends are open. One end opens to the living room, while the other end leads into the dining room and to an outdoor deck, where the Heinemeyers like to eat when the weather permits.

Ample artificial lighting keeps the kitchen bright after the sun goes down. An 8-foot fluorescent strip-light atop one row of upper cabinets shines on the ceiling, providing cool, diffused light. Fixtures mounted under the cabinets directly illuminate work areas near the cooktop and sink.

The custom-made, frameless cabinets (as well as the countertops) are surfaced with a sand-colored plastic laminate. Richard likes the "Euro-style" look because of its simple, austere lines. "There's always so much clutter that you put in a kitchen—cookbooks, pots and pans—that the cleaner the look of the cabinets, the better," he says.

This appliance garage, built into the side of the pantry, stores a blender, mixer, food processor, and knives.

To augment storage space, Richard put full-height cabinets above the refrigerator. Raising the cabinets also made room for a cookbook shelf below.

With less than 4 feet to travel from one side of the kitchen to the other, an efficient work triangle is virtually guaranteed. The cooking center, which consists of an electric cooktop and a combination oven-microwave unit, occupies half of one side of the galley; the sink and refrigerator are opposite. "It's a one-cook kitchen," admits Richard. But the cook need not be lonely. The designer/architect also managed to squeeze in a small kitchen-office area, where a second person can sit, pay bills, talk with the cook (or on the phone)—and maybe even taste the broth.

This galley kitchen, with European-style cabinetry, is long and narrow, but because it's so well-lighted and because both ends of the galley are open, it does not seem small.

Recessed pulls on the doors and drawers complement the kitchen's streamlined design; they also stay out of the cook's way. Another space-saving feature is the appliance garage built into one side of the pantry. It contains a blender, food processor, countertop mixer, and an electrical outlet so that the appliances are always plugged in and ready to use. A magnetic cutlery holder mounted on the garage door makes further use of the handy compartment.

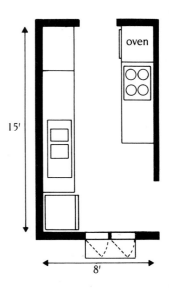

A Compact Kitchen

When Sandy and Huston Eubank moved into an apartment in Sandy's ancestral home (since 1868) in Charleston, South Carolina, the small kitchen in it hadn't been renovated in more than 40 years. It was a model of inefficiency. A hot water heater wasted an entire corner, the range and refrigerator were next to one another, countertop and cabinet space was minimal, and both the door and window opened into the room, further cramping the already skimpy space. The challenge of this remodeling was to create a functional kitchen for a family of five in a corridorlike space measuring only 7 by 10 feet.

The thick masonry walls of this house, built in the 1820s, made expanding the kitchen impractical, so the Eubanks were stuck with a small room. To create a more livable kitchen, Huston, an architect, designed a renovation that makes use of every square inch of area. "One of the first bits of research I did was to study boat galleys," he says. "That's just about the scale I was working with."

The Eubanks gutted the kitchen and started from scratch. They relocated the old door to improve circulation, reduce wasted space, and let in more light. They discarded an old, bulky refrigerator and replaced it with a Sub-Zero model because it was shallower and wider than standard refrigerators. And they moved it to the opposite side of the room to create a more efficient work triangle.

Installing a space-saver sink (in fire-engine red) created room for a dishwasher. One stock fixture they couldn't find to suit them was a range hood for their new gas range. So Huston designed his own curved version with oak trim. Using the innards of a

When every square inch of space counts, adequate storage is a big consideration. Here a drawer for towels makes good use of the corner, and the drawer for the wastebasket closes out of sight.

Thermador hood, he had a sheet-metal shop make up the hood from his drawings and an auto-body shop paint it "rangoon" red to match the sink. The result, while more

Huston Eubank studied boat galleys in order to design this efficient, 70-square-foot kitchen.

expensive than an off-the-shelf hood, adds a distinctive and colorful touch to the room.

A local architect turned cabinetmaker and his brother crafted the oak cabinets and drawers. To conserve space, the cabinets have several oversize drawers for storing pots and pans and another for a trash container. The cabinetmakers also built a matching oak-and-glass shelf under the cabinets to make the room feel more open and to display the Eubanks' favorite china. The shelves are lighted by 25-watt bulbs set in recessed plastic sockets like the ones used in bathroom mirrors. They installed a pantry cabinet for dense storage beside the refrigerator in the space that was gained because the entry door was relocated.

To steal a bit of extra space and to allow the sink and dishwasher to fit under the window, the range counter notches in to allow the door of the dishwasher to open. On the opposite side, the mechanical workings of a NuTone food processor are hidden in a dead space between cabinets. Only the power-drive spline protrudes above the countertop, awaiting attachment of the machine's various accessories.

Simplicity helps to create the feeling of a larger room. "I tried to keep the lines of the room straight and uncomplicated," says Huston. "It helps to make the space appear bigger." In addition, he used a reflective black laminate backsplash to create an illusion of depth.

The thoughtful planning that went into the redesign of this kitchen has paid off generously. While the Eubanks' kitchen will never be described as spacious, it's twice the room it used to be.

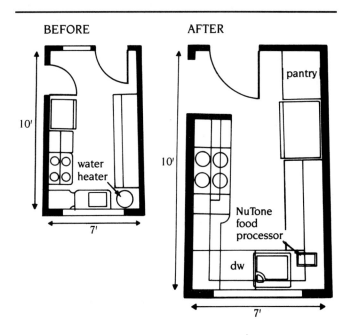

A Kitchen That
Lets the Sun Shine In

Anna and Art Fisher spent nine months planning their house with architect Sears Barrett before construction began. They knew what they wanted, but the design process was a time for refining their ideas. Since the house is on a north-facing slope, an essential design requirement was to bring as much sunlight as possible into the core of the house. "This is probably the last house we'll build," Anna says, "and we wanted it to be right." During the nine months the house was under construction, the Fishers were on site nearly every day.

After living in their two-story solar house for nine months, Anna reports that they love it. The kitchen, located on the top floor of the house, is an efficient place to work and the center of family life, as the family had hoped it would be.

One aim of the kitchen design was to get as much sunlight into the interior as possible. The kitchen borrows light from

In the Fisher kitchen there's lots of natural light from the adjoining rooms, the skylight, and the south-facing windows. At night the fluorescent tubes of the ceiling lighting fixture illuminate the space.

The pass-through serves as a convenient "buffet" for parties.

venient to the ovens and houses a cooktop—its top, made from Italian tiles, is heatproof, so hot pots won't damage it—and a trash compactor. There's enough space at the counter for friends or family to sit and talk to Anna while she is cooking. Because Anna wanted a working kitchen, not an eat-in kitchen, there is a separate dining room for family meals and more elaborate dinners. The island is strictly for quick meals.

The open shelves next to the pass-through store pottery and utensils: "If I see things, I use them, and I use my pottery a lot," Anna says. The pass-through makes serving to the living room a simple matter.

Art Fisher sells lighting fixtures, and the unusual light trough is one of his products. Fluorescent tubes throw light onto the ceiling, which bounces it back into the room.

other rooms because it is open to surrounding rooms. From the kitchen, one can look across the recessed living room to a glorious view to the north. The kitchen is easily accessible to the sunspace and hot tub and to the dining room. The result is that someone in the kitchen has ready contact with the other activity zones on the floor.

The house has 9-foot ceilings, allowing windows to extend to 8 feet up the wall. Light from the huge, barrel-vault skylight over the island moderates direct sunlight from the south-facing windows at the sink. "I always wanted windows at the sink," Anna says. The arc of the skylight repeats in the arches that lead to other rooms and in the pass-through to the living room.

The cabinets were custom-built to the Fishers' specifications. The island is con-

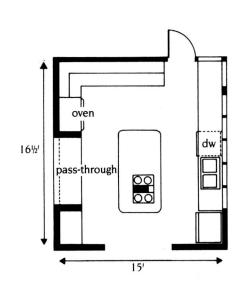

A KITCHEN OF SWIRLS AND DETAILS

John Vugrin "sculpted" the cabinets in this kitchen of curves. The work triangle is obvious. The refrigerator is convenient to both countertops. Induction tiles are recessed into the countertop opposite the rounded peninsula.

The Guth family—John, Gail, and four children—lived in their house for 18 years before they began remodeling it, and the kitchen was the last room they worked on. The original kitchen was a fairly standard, unattractive room with birch cabinets and an ugly ceramic tile backsplash, so undistinguished that the family can scarcely remember it. The new kitchen is a total change—extensive use of teak and tiles makes it a warm and inviting space, and curved tile work and counters swirl in what is a relatively tight space.

The Guths engaged architect Kendrick Bangs Kellogg to design their renovations and craftsman John Vugrin to create the cabinetry they needed. To design the kitchen, the family sat down to dinner with Kellogg and talked about the kitchen. No formal set of plans was ever drawn—Kellogg sketched details on pieces of scratch paper and laid out the cabinetry by drawing lines on the

Curves and swirls are everywhere: countertops, floors, and cabinets.

floor. It was up to Vugrin to work out the details of the cabinet design, and if he had questions, he called Kellogg.

The result is a room that is clean, warm, and rich in craftsmanly, sculptural detail. Cabinet pulls and handles are hand-carved from ebony. An open drawer reveals an inlaid red maple leaf. The curved prow of the cabinets contains wedge-shaped, hinged drawers, lined with hammered copper. A flight of geese is inlaid in the back of a wall cabinet.

Rather than installing a traditional range or cooktop, the Guths had induction tile cooktops inlaid in a countertop, flush with the tiles. These cooktops are easy to clean and cool to the touch.

The refrigerator and oven are on the wall opposite the sink. The refrigerator is convenient to two counters, and the Guths can walk right from the garage into their kitchen. From the sink, someone who is washing dishes can appreciate plants in a greenhouse window and a view of the garden. There is a built-in trash chute that empties into a bin outside the house for convenient trash disposal.

Although the entire family uses the kitchen, it is better for one person to work there at a time. Two people tend to get in each other's way.

This kitchen has some unusual lighting devices. John Vugrin built undercabinet lights right into the cabinets, and he designed the cabinets so that light is thrown up on the casings to light the insides of the cabinets. Recessed spots light the sink and sitting counter.

The dining area is adjacent to the kitchen and convenient to the large, round peninsula. This convenience and the openness of the two rooms make them the active center of the house, their warmth and sculptured curves inviting to friends and family alike.

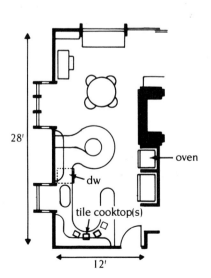

Making the Most of His Lot

People trying to squeeze the kitchen of their dreams into a frustratingly awkward space often envy those building from scratch, imagining that, for them, the sky's the limit. Consider then, the challenge that Richard Sibly faced in designing a house for his family. He had to contend with a narrow lot (60 feet wide by 280 feet deep) that was heavily wooded in the rear. Not only that,

but the long side of the lot faced due south. The result was not only a successful house (which won the 1985 Aurora Award from the Southeastern Builders Conference for the Most Energy Efficient Residential Unit) but also a successful kitchen.

Because of the orientation of the lot, his three-story solar house is long and narrow, and the kitchen is located on its first floor.

The Siblys' L-shaped kitchen juts out into the gathering room. The counter keeps people out of the cook's way but still a part of the action in the room.

A red laminate countertop and European-style cabinets create a sleek, clean look.

keeps traffic from the stairs and front door from flowing through the workspace.

An addition that Richard expects to make soon is a tambour door below the upper cabinets between the refrigerator and ovens to hide small appliances from view. Next to the ovens is a foot-deep pantry that is well used. It is always chock-full of food, and Richard wishes it were larger.

The cabinets, made in West Germany, have many built-in storage features. The cabinet cases, the insides of the drawers, and the countertops are surfaced with Duropal laminate, which has a melting point of 500°F., much higher than that of Formica.

A large, operable skylight above the kitchen washes the entire space with light during the day. It is a real boon for ventilation as well, since cooking odors and heat from the appliances can easily escape from the kitchen when the skylight is open.

Considering all the design constraints, Richard Sibly is basically satisfied with his kitchen: "I really couldn't have designed it any other way," he says. He will make some changes in his next kitchen, however. He finds the dishwasher too noisy and will make quiet operation the chief criterion for the dishwasher he installs in his next house. He also wants a larger pantry. Finally, floor-to-ceiling doors will close off a larger work area with open shelving and more counter space for appliances.

Richard wanted the kitchen to be centrally located, accessible to both the gathering room (which is used for family activities and entertaining) and the formal dining room. From the kitchen, his wife, Nancy, can see who is at the front door or look into the greenhouse.

The Sibly kitchen manages to be the center of this unusual and stylish solar house in spirit as well as fact. People seem to gather there during parties, even when a bar is set up in the greenhouse, and the three Sibly children perch atop the natural wood stools to eat breakfast at the breakfast bar. (The bar is made from a piece of oak stair tread and is trimmed in poplar, as is the rest of the house.) The L-shaped counter that juts out into the gathering room

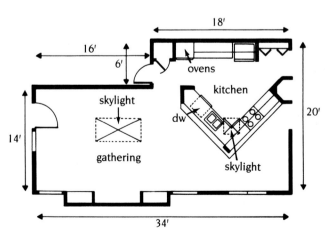

A Kitchen For A Family To Grow In

The food preparation area is ample in this kitchen, and a person working at the sink has a view of woodlands through the sunspace.

The stairway leads to a loft where the Fuller children play, always close enough to hear their mother's call.

From the sink in Joan and Peter Fuller's kitchen, one can look out through windows in the sunspace to see a quiet back road, fields, woods, and a pond. The food preparation area in this great-room kitchen is pleasant, warm, and airy. The three Fuller children and their friends munch snacks at the table or peninsula counter. Soon they'll be up the open stairs to a playroom in the loft overhead. Joan says, "I never feel stuck here. There's always a lot going on, and because the kitchen is so open, I feel as if I'm participating in everything."

This kitchen began its life about ten years ago, when the Fullers added a pas-

sive solar addition to their eighteenth-century stone farmhouse. The addition just didn't work—not only was it small and boxlike, but it overheated—so the family decided to reconstruct it, adding a sunspace, redoing the kitchen, and integrating the structure with the rest of the house.

A wealth of details makes this great room warm and inviting. Natural materials abound, including a rough-sawn post-and-beam frame, constructed from green oak cut in the Fullers' woods; handmade cabinets with cherry frames, bird's-eye maple panels, and rosewood highlights; and a random-width oak floor pegged with oak pegs and installed on a diagonal to the joists.

In planning the reconstruction, Joan and kitchen designer Suzanne G. Bates thoroughly explored how the kitchen would work. Suzanne's redesign uses all of the original cabinets; new ones were built to match by William L. McCarthy, who built the original cabinets.

The peninsula separates the kitchen work area from the living areas, allowing Joan to keep her workspace neat—a priority in a house with small children. One of the features that she most appreciates is the large butcher-block-topped "landing" beside the refrigerator—a convenient place to dump a large quantity of groceries and provisions, and just 4 feet behind the range. A covered spice cabinet above it keeps spices fresh by shutting out heat, moisture, and light.

Another practical touch is the tile inlay in the Corian countertop on the peninsula. It is a convenient place to set hot dishes for serving the family or when setting up the butcher-block sideboard in the adjacent hallway for buffet service to the formal dining room.

The kitchen features several built-in storage units, including a large pantry, two lazy Susans, and a cookbook shelf. Joan stores the attachments for the Jenn-Air in a cabinet next to the range.

The reason the Fullers' kitchen is so satisfying is that it now works. The open space will allow other uses as the family grows older. Designed to be a place for the entire family, it has indeed become the hub around which family life revolves.

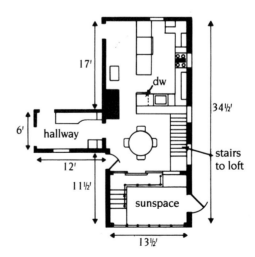

This handcrafted walnut sideboard has an oak and walnut butcher-block top. The sideboard is in a hallway next to the kitchen and provides buffet service to the formal dining room.

A Study in Contrasts

Carl Gable says jokingly that his wife, Louise, dreamed about her ideal kitchen for a year before she even talked to him about it. She had very definite ideas about what she wanted and a stack of clippings collected from magazines over a period of ten years or so. The result of such long-term planning is a striking black and white kitchen that incorporates some unusual storage ideas.

The Gables wanted a European-style kitchen with plenty of built-in storage. But, more importantly, they wanted a place where friends could gather, and where they could sit down to meals with children and grandchildren. They had become increasingly frustrated with their small kitchen, small dining room, and large rec room and wanted to replace them with one room that would serve three functions.

Craig Bomboy was a logical choice as kitchen designer—he had designed two bathrooms for the Gables and could construct exactly what they wanted in his well-equipped shop. Furthermore, he was innovative enough to work out design problems encountered in fabricating the unusual custom cabinets in this kitchen. Planning the kitchen took three months of discussions, phone calls, and rough sketches before the Gables settled on a final plan.

The biggest problem Bomboy faced was obtaining the cabinet hardware he needed; most of it came from hard-to-locate sources in Europe. For example, the slides for the appliance garages had to be ordered

With high-tech European cabinetry, this black and white kitchen is right in style. Lots of appliance garages and energy-efficient appliances make this a smart kitchen in every way.

106

The cabinetry in this kitchen has lots of hidden storage options, including roll-out wire racks and pull-out shelves.

from Austria. The hardware often came without assembly or installation instructions and required metric tools. The cabinet cases themselves had to be built to much more exacting tolerances than American cabinets usually are, which is typical of most European-style cabinets.

The kitchen took nine months to construct. During construction—"the upstairs was all torn up," the Gables say—they cooked in a small kitchen in their basement.

One of the innovative features in this kitchen is the appliance garages that line one counter on the island. Each garage has a pull-out lower shelf, making the appliances very easy to use. Outlets are hidden in the back of the garages.

The exhaust hood over the cooktop is a space-age attention-getter. It was custom-fabricated from stainless steel and painted with a flat black epoxy.

With so much planning and forethought, the Gables find that they are satisfied with the kitchen of their dreams. Would they make any changes? Carl Gable says no,

then pauses: "If I had to do it over again, I might put in a marble floor." The Gables rejected a black-and-white-tiled marble floor originally planned for the kitchen because of structural and cost reasons.

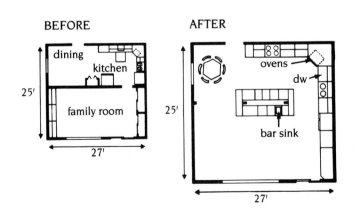

A Grand Country Kitchen

Barbara and David Bollinger's 100 acres in eastern Pennsylvania afford a perfect setting for a grand stone farmhouse. Their three-story re-creation, built of native stone, resembles an old farmhouse, yet contains contemporary conveniences.

Barbara carried the farmhouse theme into the kitchen she designed herself. "My husband loves country—but I like contemporary style, too," Barbara says. Their kitchen blends both influences—while rich in details that evoke historical connections, it lacks the clutter often associated with the country look.

The Bollinger kitchen functions as a very practical workspace. "I knew my work habits and the way I move in the kitchen, so I designed this kitchen to do what I wanted,"

Finely crafted pine cabinets, ceiling beams from Vermont, and stenciling on the walls are a few of the details that contribute to the country feeling in this kitchen.

A pine table, Windsor chairs, and a hutch filled with antique glassware make dining in this kitchen a visual delight.

Barbara explains. She worked closely with a local cabinetmaker who built the cabinets, sometimes from verbal descriptions of what she wanted. "He was great to work with, because if I didn't like something, he'd take it out and redo it," she says. Her cabinets of solid pine have pull-out shelves and drawers lined with Formica to make them easier to clean.

The location of the large island relative to the refrigerator, wall ovens, and cooktop is integral to making the kitchen a convenient place to work. Barbara can set hot dishes from the oven on either the cooktop or on trivets placed on the almond-colored Corian countertop. Setting groceries on the island makes loading the refrigerator or voluminous pantry an easy task.

There is plenty of storage in the kitchen cabinets, in the hutch, and in a large built-in cabinet in the dining area. Because Barbara Bollinger is short, she had her wall cabinets dropped to 14 inches above the countertops, allowing easy access to the top shelves.

The strong architectural features in the kitchen contribute to its country feeling. Hand-hewn pine beams from Vermont (the Bollingers chose new beams because the

old barn beams they wanted to use were infested with insects) support a ceiling of random-width planks with beaded edges. The floor is tiled with Mexican tiles, one of which retains the imprint of a goat's hoof left while the tile was sun-drying. Antiques and collectibles round out the decor of this grand farmhouse kitchen, as do details like the subtle stencil borders on the walls.

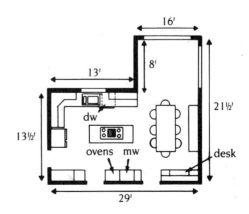

109

A Kitchen by the Sea

Striking wallpaper in an Egyptian palm motif does much to set the mood in this kitchen.

The house of Carol and Stan Danowitz is, in a manner of speaking, surrounded by the sea. Built on a coastal island, it is separated from the Atlantic Ocean by a salt marsh. The house is built on pilings 5 feet off the ground to meet federal floodplain regulations.

The interior of the house is designed so that its spaces flow into one another,

making the house appear larger than it is. Vaulted ceilings contribute to the feeling of spaciousness. Skylights and windows bring natural light into the house—and allow people inside to appreciate views of woods or ocean.

The kitchen is an open, cheerful room. There's a glass table in one corner for breakfast and informal dining, and the ocean is

buffets and for serving to the dining room.

Glass surrounds the kitchen: the glass doors to the porch, windows over the sink that permit a view of the woods outside, and three 2-by-2-foot skylights that allow sunlight to filter into the room.

When the house was framed, studs in the wall behind the refrigerator were installed on the flat so that the front of the refrigerator would be flush with the cabinet fronts. A notch was framed into the wall next to the dishwasher for the microwave.

The Danowitzes have plenty of counter space in their kitchen and, despite the lack of wall space, plenty of storage in the cabinets. The cabinets feature roll-out shelves, and the corner cabinet has turn-out shelves. The cabinets are European-style, with a frameless construction, and feature under-cabinet fluorescents built into the cabinets by the manufacturer. This not only allows all countertops to be well-lighted but also allows a neat appearance on the bottoms of the wall cabinets.

The Danowitzes get many compliments on their kitchen—it's the place where people gather during parties—and the Danowitzes themselves couldn't be happier with their kitchen by the sea.

A vaulted ceiling and skylights create a feeling of spaciousness in this kitchen. The butcher-block island functions as a gathering point for guests at the Danowitzes' parties.

visible through the sliding glass doors that open onto a screened porch. A door leads into the dining room and living room. The unusual wallpaper with its Egyptian palm motif adds to the beauty of the room.

The kitchen, indeed the entire house, is perfect for the informal style of entertaining the Danowitzes prefer. (Having parties is a major focus of social life on the island where they live.) A bar and wine rack in the kitchen allows do-it-yourself serving, and the large central island does not contain a cooktop or sink because it was specifically intended to act as a serving area, both for

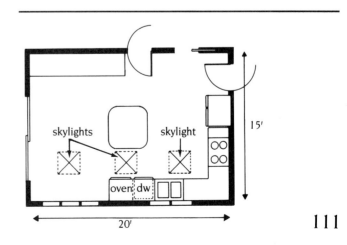

A RESPECT FOR TRADITION

The house Pat and David Sydney bought in a small Pennsylvania town looked at first like something out of "The Munsters." A gloomy brick Victorian, the house had been totally neglected. Worst of all was the kitchen. Located at the rear of the first floor, the kitchen was a dreary, inefficient workspace that lacked modern appliances and counters.

With the help of Harry Williams, an ex-perienced builder/remodeler, the Sydneys set to work designing a new kitchen. "We wanted a contemporary kitchen, but we wanted it to echo the Victorian character of the house," says Pat.

Williams began the transformation by gutting the space. Next, he cast an experienced eye on the floor plan. In the original floor plan, a woodstove, sink, gas range,

This contemporary kitchen successfully captures the character of the Victorian house. The cabinets, of tongue-and-groove wainscoting, are in the same style as the Victorian woodwork.

This pass-through opens to a sunspace, a room that is very much a part of how the kitchen works.

and refrigerator were scattered about the room with no apparent rhyme or reason. Williams suggested a U-shaped layout for the kitchen work area.

In designing new cabinets, Pat took her cue from existing Victorian woodwork. "The old kitchen had a small section of tongue-and-groove wainscoting along part of the wall—a typically Victorian feature that had given character to the old kitchen and one that I hoped to incorporate in some way," says Pat. "It was not possible to just add more, since today it is made in a different width. So we wainscoted the sitting area with new material and repeated the tongue-and-groove paneling in the cabinet doors," notes Pat, a trained art historian.

The cabinets are as practical as they are pretty. A flip-down drawer underneath the sink stores sponges, brushes, and cleansers. A tall, narrow drawer next to the stove is actually a pull-out spice rack. An iron pot rack, overhanging the cooktop, puts pots and pans conveniently within the cook's reach and saves shelf space.

The new, compact workspace is tucked into a corner of the old kitchen. The Sydneys

furnished the space on the northern end of the room with a couch and a woodstove, creating a cozy sitting room. When they renovated the kitchen, they added a sunspace along the south wall. Today this pleasant trio of rooms is the center of family life.

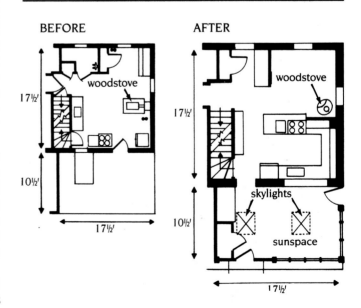

A KITCHEN PERSONALIZED FOR THE LONG TERM

Retaining the windows meant giving up space for cabinets, but Linda and Tom Gettings willingly did this so the kitchen would get lots of light.

The kitchen in the home of Linda and Tom Gettings, like the rest of their 1903 Tudor Revival house, reflects the very personal attention of its owners. So far, remodeling the kitchen has taken 14 months, with a few additions yet to come. There have been inconveniences. But because the family intends to stay in this house for a long time, what counts is creating a kitchen that will be as pleasing 15 years from now as it is today.

"We never could have done what we did without Richard," states Tom. Tom credits Richard Weinsteiger, who built the cabinets and did the carpentry in the kitchen, with making the owners' ideas work. "I encourage people to work with the artisans in their area. Many times, they give you exactly what you want at a cost comparable to that of a factory-made custom kitchen," Tom says.

Getting what you want involves knowing what you want. Designing their kitchen meant living in the house before changing it. And it meant getting involved in some of the work—Tom spent four months "depinking" the old kitchen, stripping layers of pink paint off of old cabinets and moldings. The result is lovely: original birch cabinets and paneled doors. (Richard refaced the cabinets in the sink area with new doors and drawer fronts to match the old cabinetry.)

Because the six doors and two windows in the kitchen kept it open, light, and airy, Linda and Tom decided to retain them, even though it meant giving up cabinet and countertop space. Some of their dishes and glassware have found a home in the cabinet in the butler's pantry, which also serves as a bar—another original feature that Tom depinked.

The 2-by-3-foot butcher-block island is the main food preparation area and, in

Friends and family alike gather around the table at the other end of the kitchen to talk or watch TV.

The cabinets to the left of the door were stripped of ugly pink paint to reveal lovely birch cabinets. The cabinets to the right of the door were stripped, too, and new doors to match those on the left were installed. A new floor, ceiling, butcher-block island, and red tile countertop make this a totally new kitchen.

The grimness of this kitchen before remodeling is obvious in this "before" photograph.

effect, divides the space in the kitchen between workspace and living space. The island is effectively lighted by a custom-built fixture with paneled sides; it houses fluorescents. Two hanging Victorian lamps, which Tom assembled from parts purchased from several mail-order sources, provide task lighting over the sink and range.

The countertop on the island and around the sink is butcher block. The red tile on the other counters runs up the walls and is complemented by a row of decorative tiles that Tom hand-selected at a local tile works. Beaded, tongue-and-groove mahogany, custom-milled in Richard's shop, covers the ceiling. Carefully chosen wallpaper echoes more elaborately papered walls elsewhere in the house.

Still to come is a cabinet that will link the range and refrigerator (which, in the redesigning, was moved to the small room adjacent to the kitchen) and provide more counter space and house a microwave oven.

The result of the evolutionary planning of this kitchen is a room that is functional, yet warm enough to attract family and friends.

"We have this huge Victorian house—but everyone ends up in the kitchen," Linda says. What's more, its design is completely satisfying to its owners, who wouldn't change a thing.

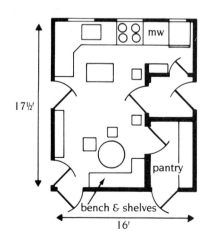

A KITCHEN
WITH A SOUND VIEW

The Salyers gladly sacrificed upper cabinets in their kitchen so that they would have a perfect view of Puget Sound. There is plenty of storage space elsewhere in the kitchen.

The Salyer kitchen, located in a remodeled Seattle beach cottage, has a sound view of the world. From their kitchen windows, Dolores and Phil Salyer watch freighters, military vessels, and pleasure boats in Puget Sound, one of the West Coast's busiest shipping lanes. Their kitchen is surrounded by windows to take fullest advantage of the ever-changing views. The house has a 210-degree southern view, encompassing Mount Rainier, Puget Sound, and the Olympic Mountains.

The community in which they live is much like California's Sausalito, Dolores says. A mixed neighborhood, its eclectic mix of residents are, like the Salyers, transforming old cottages into striking living spaces. The Salyer house is a one-room beach cottage, built in 1928, which has had additions added throughout the past five decades. The challenge they faced was to take this hodgepodge structure and make it work as an integrated living space.

Architect Allen D. Elliot created a five-

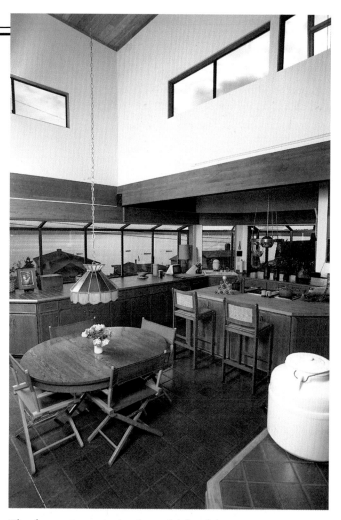

level dwelling with open spaces inside, plenty of windows (south-facing glass provides significant solar gain), and numerous decks. The Seattle *Times* and the Seattle chapter of the American Institute of Architects, recently chose this as the House of the Month.

The openness of the interior allows guests to move from one area of the house to another. The house is great for parties. (Dolores's son calls it a "full-on, raging party house.") The Salyers, who entertain frequently, have hosted as many as 140 people.

Their kitchen fits right into their lifestyle. Like the house and the Salyers themselves, it is open and generous, inviting guests to share food, hospitality, and views. They use the huge, irregularly shaped island as a serving area or for dining. Oak stools allow friends to sit and talk to people working in the kitchen. Dolores bought the Jenn-Air cooktop at a garage sale; it was brand new.

Carlos Sabich, an Argentinian craftsman, custom-built the oak cabinets for the Salyers. Dolores loves the exquisitely detailed cabinets—Sabich matched the grain on the cabinet fronts and carefully adjusted the doors so they close at a touch.

Despite the lack of overhead cabinets, there is plenty of storage room in the base cabinets, the island, and the tall cabinets beside the ovens. Workspace is also ample: Extra-wide, tile-covered counters extend all the way into the greenhouse windows. The tiles have a matte finish, and the counters are trimmed in oak.

The Salyers enjoy their kitchen to the fullest. Is it perfect? Not quite—Dolores, if she were doing the kitchen again, would want morning sunshine in the kitchen. But she always appreciates her sound view.

The large, irregularly shaped island has many purposes: It houses a cooktop; it's a place for informal dining; it makes the kitchen triangle compact; and it's a place to visit with friends.

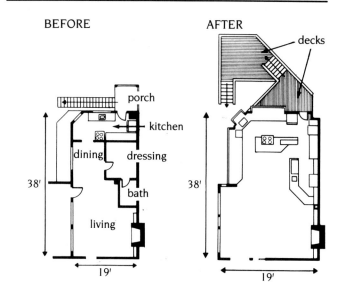

BEFORE

AFTER

decks

porch

kitchen

dining

dressing

bath

living

38'

19'

38'

19'

A KITCHEN WITH A GARDEN VIEW

June and William Hall, the owners of this kitchen, credit designer Richard Elmore with a successful design. The Richard Elmore Design firm turned a tiny kitchen into one that allows people in the food preparation area to talk to others in the adjacent family room and to appreciate a view of the garden outside. But Elmore says, "They can give me all the credit they want, but you can't have good results without a good client. A client is 90 percent responsible for whatever level of success there is!"

The Halls are a successful professional couple with two children. They are the fourth owners of their 25-year-old, custom-designed house. The original kitchen was not only tiny, but someone at the sink washing dishes looked out into a carport. The Halls enjoy entertaining, but their old kitchen couldn't accommodate guests, and the existing family room was too small. The designers added just 300 square feet of space to 700 square feet of existing space—but what a difference it made!

Richard Elmore turned a small kitchen into a large one and successfully created space for a variety of activities: cooking, lounging, partying, watching TV, and dining.

Standing at this sink, one has a view of the great-room kitchen and the garden and patio.

A gently curving peninsula houses the sink, dishwasher, and cooktop. Now someone can work at the cooktop or sink and look outside to the patio and garden. Stools at the peninsula counter allow family or guests to talk to someone in the kitchen. There's even room for a table in the kitchen, which can serve as an additional work area or be used for family meals. As part of the renovation, the Halls added a desk and shelves against the wall immediately behind the cooktop to serve as their home computer center.

The newly expanded family room is not only the center of family activities but also a room that is filled with light. The large windows, oriented to 10-degrees west of south, provide solar gain and the dark-colored tiles on the floor act as a heat sink. Track lights in the ceiling light the family room, and lights recessed in the curved soffit light the counter and kitchen. The Elmore firm prefers to have too much light in a room than not enough; they even make sure that the floor is well-lighted. A skylight in the center of the kitchen brings daylight into what would otherwise be an enclosed space.

Several design elements in this room make both the kitchen and family room seem larger than they are. The curved peninsula lends a sculptural, contemporary feeling to the room, is easy to move around, and actually takes less space from the family room than a right-angled peninsula would. The cathedral ceiling in the family room contributes an additional feeling of spaciousness.

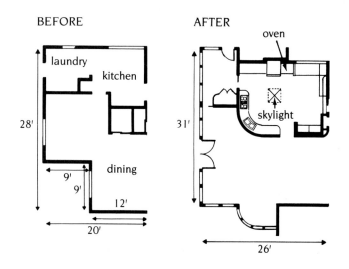

Rescuing a Poor Design

The windows in the Teufel kitchen open it up to the beauty of the outdoors. The large, tile-covered island is the hub of activity for both family and social life.

"Why did we redo the kitchen of a new house that we have lived in for five years?" Ann Teufel asks. "Because it was a stupid design." Designing a kitchen that didn't work was one mistake the original architect made in Ann and Robert Teufel's house. Among other features, it had a very small island and a space-wasting and completely useless pantry. Ann wanted a great-room kitchen that both family and friends could enjoy. So, the Teufels redid the original kitchen,

replacing it with one that is convenient, attractive, and satisfying, and one that serves as a family room. It's not uncommon for the family to watch TV while Ann cooks, or for friends to sit at the table or stand at the island to visit.

The "new" kitchen is the result of a collaboration between Robert Wieland, CKD, and Iris Konia, an interior designer. They were given free rein, and Ann credits them with the many special touches that make

Lots of windows in this kitchen mean that wall space for storage is limited. The solution is cabinetry with many unique storage options behind the cabinet doors.

used for a three-shelf, above-the-counter lazy Susan.

A section of counter spans a window and allows plenty of room next to the sink. Originally, there were only a few inches of room here. Ann can stand at the sink and look out onto a lovely wooded view; the family pet has a cat's-eye view of the same scene when she eats dinner from dishes set on the floor underneath this counter.

The central island was enlarged to allow more space beside the cooktop. It houses a Jenn-Air cooktop and a pull-out trash can. It also functions as a serving area for buffets and as a bar for parties. Ann appreciates pulling hot pots off the range and being able to set them on the heatproof tiles.

Iris created a baking center by mounting a microwave oven next to the twin conventional ovens. Ann stores pans and equipment for use in the microwave oven in the cabinet above it.

The Teufels have their great-room kitchen at last—a pleasing workspace and a warm family room. The only change Ann would make is to bump out a wall to add a place for a couch and chair. Her advice to those who are building new homes is to find an expert who knows about good kitchen design. Don't accept the lowest bid. "In the end, you get what you pay for," she says.

her kitchen work. For example, Iris suggested inlaying a cutting board in the tile counter to the right of the sink; it is easy to clean and always handy. A wooden cutting board for vegetables pulls out of a drawer to the left of the sink. A long slot cut into the back of the counter near the sink holds knives. A KitchenAid mixer pulls out from underneath the counter; its accessories are stored underneath.

Wieland added many ingenious storage features in the kitchen. A telephone had previously occupied the wall opposite the sink, which could not accept standard cabinets because they would block traffic. Now a foot-deep pantry, which stores canned goods and dried foods, occupies that space but allows people to pass freely. Once-wasted space to the left of the refrigerator was

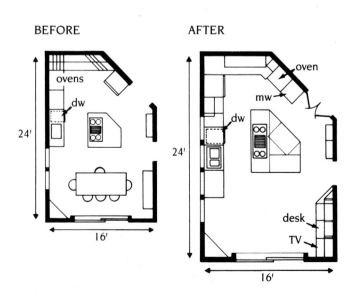

DAVID'S KITCHEN

The home of Linda and David Ziegenfuss is a one-room schoolhouse that they completely renovated. Visitors admire the stonework or the open-beam ceilings and remark at how attractive the house is. Until Linda points out its many unique design features, many people don't even notice that this house was built to be accessible to David, who is confined to a wheelchair.

That was Linda's intention when she designed the house. "Disabled people like nice things, too," she says. The process of designing a house for someone who is disabled requires attention to details that the rest of us take for granted every day. Linda researched house design for the handicapped and then realized that she had to come up with her own design to make a kitchen inviting as well as functional. She rejected the institutional appearance of many kitchens designed for the disabled. "This is David's home, not a hospital," she says.

She recommends that a house be designed for the individual who will use it. Before completing her kitchen design, Linda brought David's wheelchair to the house and did a dry run in the kitchen, making sure that she had planned everything correctly.

The kitchen Linda settled upon is a simple galley plan with refrigerator, range,

At first glance, it is not obvious that this kitchen is easily accessible to David, who is confined to a wheelchair. The sink, range, and cabinet beside the refrigerator are lower than standard cabinet height.

David uses this countertop to prepare food. The microwave oven, recessed into the wall, is close at hand. Here's a unique use of upper cabinets: They form the *base* for this countertop.

and sink on one wall. David uses the kitchen extensively to prepare meals, and almost everything is within reach from his wheelchair. Although Linda is usually the one who uses the overhead cabinets, David is able to reach into these cabinets with a grabber. The countertop at the sink was dropped from standard height to 31¼ inches from the floor, making it easier for David to use. (The other countertop is standard height because it has to accommodate the dishwasher.) Linda chose a Jenn-Air range because it was the only model she could find that could be installed at less than standard cabinet height, and because it has controls on the front panel—David doesn't have to reach over a hot burner to adjust its heat. The side-by-side refrigerator, with its long handles, is easy for him to open.

Linda decided to use two standard upper cabinets (30 inches tall and 12 inches deep) instead of standard base cabinets (34½ inches tall and 24 inches deep) to support the countertop on the opposite wall, which David uses for preparing meals. This clever arrangement eliminated the need to have cabinets built especially to accommodate a countertop that is less than standard depth. The area underneath the sink is open, allowing David to pull up his wheelchair to clean vegetables or wash dishes. The cabinet next to the dishwasher stores pots and pans. Dishes are stored above

the dishwasher; when David sets the table, someone takes the dishes out of the cabinets for him. The brick floor and the distance between the counters make it easy for David to turn his wheelchair.

A mark of thoughtful design is that this kitchen works equally well when Linda uses it. What's more important is that it looks like a normal kitchen. As Linda says, "Anyone could live here and use this kitchen. We are unique, but we try to keep things 'normal looking' but functional for our special needs."

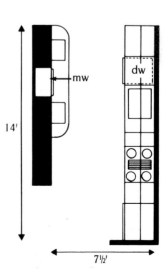

123

A KITCHEN WITH CONTEMPORARY CURVES

When Cheryl and Larry Williams began thinking about remodeling the kitchen of their four-bedroom suburban colonial, they had simply planned to make it more efficient. But just before they signed the contracts, they decided to start over and design a kitchen that contained everything they *really* wanted. Since the kitchen of their dreams didn't fit into their old house, they bumped out the back wall of their house, replacing an unused deck with 320 square feet of additional space.

The result is a sleek, contemporary kitchen with efficient workspace, plenty of storage, and not one square corner. The cabinets, European style with an unusual design, are available with both square and rounded corners. The Williamses selected the latter for a more contemporary appearance. The cabinets were installed so that no

This great-room kitchen has everything: a food preparation area, an office area, a dining area, an entertainment center, and a view to the greenery outdoors.

Curves in laminate cabinetry are the very latest trend in kitchen design, and this kitchen shows this to perfection. The white laminate cabinets are highlighted with silver trim and pulls.

hinges or fasteners are visible; special moldings hold the curved back of the island in place so that no fasteners show. Unobtrusive brushed chrome handles and pulls blend into the trim strips on cabinet doors and drawer fronts.

The kitchen is a truncated L-shape, with the dining area, a TV, and stereo located on the smaller end of the "L," which allows the two Williams children to wash dishes and watch TV. Speakers for the stereo are built into the soffits, which curve to match the curves in the counters. (Building the curved soffits was the most difficult part of the job.)

The Char-Glo barbecue is separated from the sink and cooktop, allowing Larry to work there while Cheryl prepares the rest of a meal. All four members of the family can easily use the kitchen at once without getting in each other's way. The hood over the Char-Glo echoes the one over the Whirlpool cooktop. The bar is located next to the ovens, keeping activity there during parties out of the main area of the kitchen.

The cabinets feature pull-out shelves and even have a stepladder built into one of the toe-kick spaces. A floor-to-ceiling corner cabinet, covered by a curved door, contains two lazy Susans. A planning desk has open shelves above it for cookbooks.

The smoothly curving island contains

the cleanup areas and yards of countertop. It directs traffic out of the main work areas. The gas cooktop and refrigerator are built into the cabinet right across from it. The Sub-Zero refrigerator has an exterior of Formica with brushed chrome to match the cabinets.

The Williams family is completely satisfied with their dream kitchen—it has the exact appearance they wanted, and it is a dream to work in. Cheryl says, "There isn't anything in the kitchen I have misgivings about."

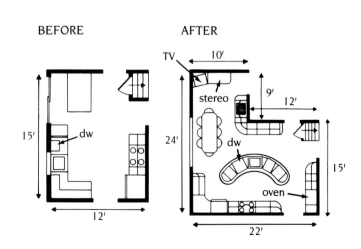

BEFORE   AFTER

125

WORKBOOK
THE BASICS OF KITCHEN DESIGN

DESIGNING YOUR NEW KITCHEN

Anyone who is planning a kitchen must make dozens of decisions, from choice of appliances to placement of lighting fixtures. Some involve spending hundreds, and even thousands, of dollars. Others cost less but are of equal importance. The more attention paid to making decisions, both large and small, the more satisfying the end result.

Other chapters of this book have emphasized decision making and have enumerated some of the *many* options you have when planning a kitchen. This chapter is different.

Most sections of this chapter concentrate on nitty-gritty details, such as standard cabinet and appliance sizes. We've avoided details like these elsewhere in this book, emphasizing design concepts and ideas instead. But the information contained in this chapter is important in making concepts and ideas work.

This chapter is vital to anyone who wants a new kitchen, even those who will engage professionals to execute and carry through a design. The more carefully you plan your kitchen, the more thoroughly you understand what you have and what you want, the better the result will be. We can't emphasize too strongly that the owners of the very successful kitchens in this book were involved in every step of the process, had definite ideas about what they wanted, and clearly articulated them to designers and tradespeople alike.

Envision this chapter, then, as a tool kit. Use the tools it contains to help appraise your present kitchen and to guide you in conceiving the kitchen of your dreams. The section on contracts is also important. Drawing up clear, concise, and correct contracts with designers and tradespeople is an important, but often neglected, detail. A contract provides a framework for determining who is responsible for what, when, and in what condition, and it outlines a schedule of payments. A contract helps to clarify relationships and to clear up misunderstandings, keeping the flow of work as smooth as possible.

Following this chapter we have included a list of manufacturers for your convenience. (See "Helpful Addresses.") Before buying any major appliance or any component of your new kitchen, you should do your homework. Comparing prices, styles, and performance will ensure that you make wise investments.

How to Use an Architectural Scale

An architectural scale—one of those funny-looking triangular rulers covered with numbers—will make it much easier for you to do an accurate scale drawing of your kitchen. You can buy one for as little as $4 at a good art-supply store.

Beverly Wilson recommends drawing kitchens at a scale of ½ inch to the foot. You'll find that scale marked at the right end of your architectural scale. Directly below the number "½," you will see "⅛" (upside down). At the left end of the same face will be "1," with "¼" right underneath. Finding these other numbers simply helps you find the right section of the ruler; the only scale you'll need right now is the one marked "½."

An architectural scale is a useful tool to use when making a drawing of your new kitchen.

Starting at the "½" and reading across from right to left, you'll see a series of numbers—0, 2, 4, 6, and so forth—close to the top edge of the ruler. Those numbers represent feet in a drawing done at a scale of ½ inch to the foot. At that scale, a line drawn from the "0" to the "4"—2 inches long in your drawing—would correspond to a distance of 4 feet in your kitchen. Pay no attention to the 10, 9, 8, 7, and so forth that fall in between the 0, 2, 4, 6; those are for drawing to a different scale—1 inch to the foot—and read from the other end of the ruler. At the scale of ½ inch to the foot, the line at "10" is really "1"; the line at "9" is really "3"; and so on.

To the right of the "0" are a series of tiny lines very close together. Each line represents ½ inch. For example, to draw a line that stands for a distance of 51 inches, start by thinking of it as 4 feet, 3 inches. Place the number "4" on the spot you're measuring from. A line from there to "0" represents 4 feet. Then measure 6 fine lines past the "0" and make a dot on your drawing. A line drawn from the starting point to that dot will represent 51 inches, at a scale of ½ inch to the foot.

One note of caution: Don't use your architectural scale as a straightedge; you'll wear down the edge.

How to Use an Architectural Template

An architectural template is a remarkably useful, inexpensive tool that will simplify the task of designing your kitchen. You can buy a kitchen and bath template at the same place you buy your architectural scale. (Kitchen symbols are sometimes found on

The cutouts on an architectural template make it easy to add important elements to the drawing of your new kitchen.

a general architectural template.) Buy one in the scale to which you are drawing your kitchen. (We recommend ½ inch to the foot.)

The cutouts milled into each template represent appliances, cabinet runs, door swings, sinks, and other important architectural elements in the kitchen—in the different sizes available, and to scale, with allowance for the width of a pencil point in tracing!

Using a template is simple. When you want to draw in your range, for example, find the cutout that represents the size range you will use. Place the template on the drawing, aligning it using the alignment marks (sometimes hair-thin lines, sometimes dots). Then trace the outline of the range on your drawing.

Cabinetry

The standardization of heights, widths, and sizes has simplified buying factory-made kitchen cabinets. Even custom-made cabinets adhere to these measurements, unless they are built for a particularly unusual area. The illustration opposite provides standard cabinet sizes and counter depths.

Remember that these are standards only, and you may deviate from them. If you're tall, you may want to elevate most of your base cabinets a few inches to make working at the countertops easier. (However, if you will soon sell your home, you would be wise to install the cabinets at standard height.) If you are short, you may want to drop not only your base cabinets but also your upper cabinets. (Again, if you are considering selling your home soon, you could drop just the upper cabinets because it is easy to move them to standard height.) Many cooks who are short drop wall cabinets to 15 inches from the counter.

Standard base cabinets vary in width, allowing flexibility in layout, and upper cabinets vary in height. They can be easily sized to fit ceiling height, which can vary from the 8-foot height common in new construction to 7 feet in old houses or to higher ceilings in some Victorian houses.

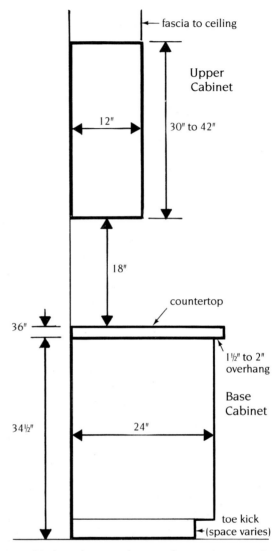

Your kitchen does not have to fit together exactly like this, but these are the standard dimensions and locations of kitchen cabinets.

Kitchen Corners

The corners of the kitchen where cabinets meet demand close scrutiny. An ideal kitchen would probably not have any corners in it, but in reality most kitchens do. Corners always present a problem in kitchen design; if they are poorly planned, drawers or doors to cabinets or appliances won't open properly. In contrast, it's possible to gain valuable storage space by fully using the space inside corner cabinets, space that will be lost if the corners are ignored.

There are a number of ways to ensure that corner space is used for maximum

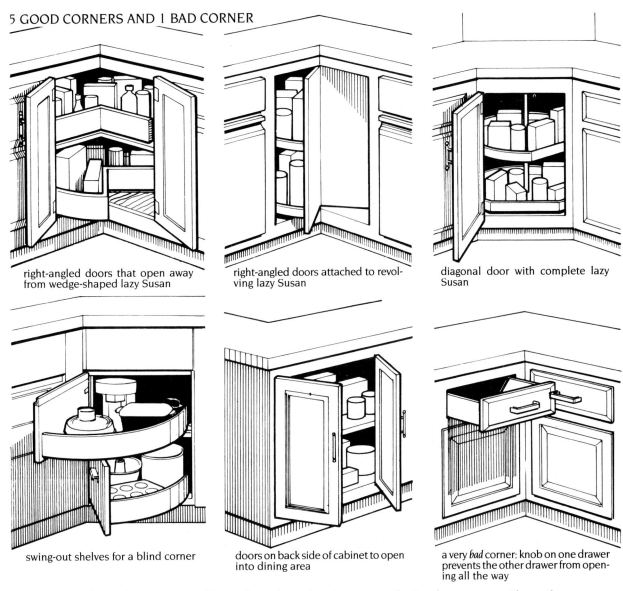

right-angled doors that open away from wedge-shaped lazy Susan

right-angled doors attached to revolving lazy Susan

diagonal door with complete lazy Susan

swing-out shelves for a blind corner

doors on back side of cabinet to open into dining area

a very *bad* corner; knob on one drawer prevents the other drawer from opening all the way

Corners in kitchen cabinetry are problems if you don't plan them properly. Good corners provide easily accessible storage space, while bad corners create nearly useless storage space.

storage. The illustration above shows five ways to use this space well and one example of what happens when corners are not properly planned. Three of the examples use lazy Susans. In one, the cabinets have right-angled doors that open away from a revolving, wedge-shaped lazy Susan. In another, right-angled doors are attached to the lazy Susan so that the doors revolve when the cabinet is opened. A disadvantage of this lazy Susan is that it is easy to catch your fingers between the doors and the cabinet. A third kind has a diagonal door with a completely revolving lazy Susan behind.

Swing-out shelves are a very convenient storage system for corner cabinetry. Because they swing out, there is no possibility that objects will be lost from sight. Swing-out shelves are especially good for storing pots and pans.

If a corner cabinet is adjacent to a dining area, this cabinet can open into that area rather than into the kitchen. The corner cabinet is then a handy storage space for linens, dishware, candlesticks, and silverware.

Sinks can be installed in corners, but

131

SINK PLACEMENT

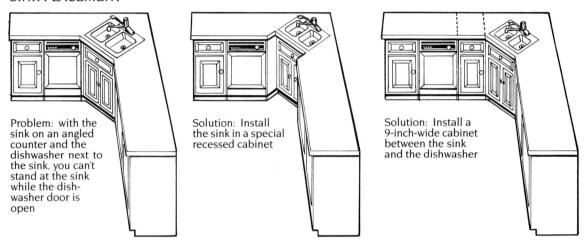

Problem: with the sink on an angled counter and the dishwasher next to the sink, you can't stand at the sink while the dish-washer door is open

Solution: Install the sink in a special recessed cabinet

Solution: Install a 9-inch-wide cabinet between the sink and the dishwasher

Above are two examples of ways to place a sink in a corner.

again it is necessary to plan this carefully. For example, if a sink is placed at an angle in a corner with a dishwasher next to it, it will be impossible to easily stand at the sink when the dishwasher is open, a stance that is common when doing kitchen cleanup. The illustration above shows two solutions to this problem.

Appliances should not be installed too close to a corner, because this arrangement makes it impossible to open some

cabinet drawers. Who is going to open the oven in order to open a drawer, as in the illustration on page 133? And, if you wedge a refrigerator into a corner, it will be impossible to fully open the door and to pull out the bins.

Bad corners find their way into kitchens, but in every example that we've seen, it was simply a case of poor planning. Some extra consideration in the planning process will result in this space being utilized sensibly.

2 BAD CORNERS

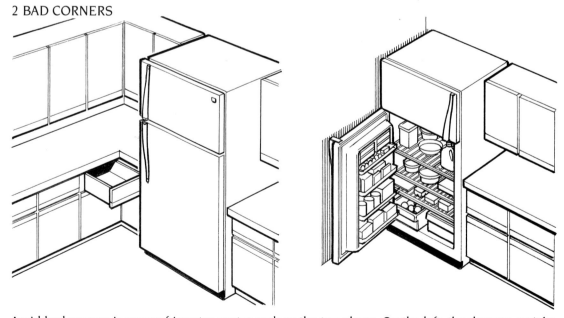

Avoid bad corners in your refrigerator center such as the two above. On the left, the drawers can't be opened more than 15 inches. On the right, the refrigerator is wedged into a corner. As a result, the door doesn't fully open and the handle hits the wall. Also, the refrigerator's vegetable drawers and shelves can't slide out.

A BAD CORNER

Avoid bad corners in your range center such as the one above. The cabinet drawer runs into the oven-door handle. As a result, the oven door has to be open for the drawer to pass.

Kitchen Work Centers

There are three basic work centers in the kitchen triangle: the refrigerator center, the sink center, and the range center. Each center performs a distinct role and provides storage for the activities that take place there. The sink center plays the most central role in relation to the other two centers and therefore should be located so that it is convenient to the other two centers (in most cases between them). For efficiency it is desirable to locate the refrigerator near the entrance to the kitchen and the range near the dining area.[1]

The Sink Center

The sink center (for food preparation, cleaning, and cleanup) provides storage for everyday dishes, glassware, pots and pans, cutlery, silver, pitchers and shakers, vegetable bins, linen, towel rack, wastebasket, cleaning materials, and utensils, garbage can or disposal, and dishdrain. Some codes require louvers or other venting provision in the doors under enclosed sinks.

Trash Compactor: Undercounter or Freestanding

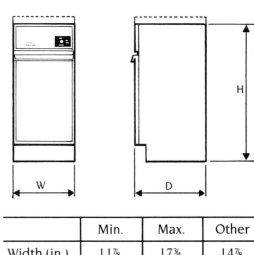

	Min.	Max.	Other
Width (in.)	11⅞	17¾	14⅞
Depth (in.)	18	24³⁄₁₆	18¼
Height (in.)	33½	35	34½

1. The information about kitchen work centers on pp. 133-37 is reprinted, by permission of John Wiley & Sons, from *Architectural Graphic Standards*, 7th ed., Robert T. Packard, ed., copyright © 1981 by John Wiley & Sons. The illustrations on these pages are redrawn from *Architectural Graphic Standards* by permission of John Wiley & Sons.

SINK CENTER
(food preparation,
cleaning, and cleanup)

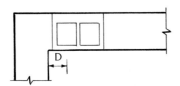

D = 14″ min.

D = clearance between the center of the sink bowl
and the turn of the counter

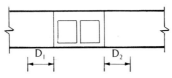

D_1 = 18″ to 36″

D_2 = 24″ to 36″

Provide workspace on both sides of sink; if dishwasher is used, allow at least 24″ to the right or
left

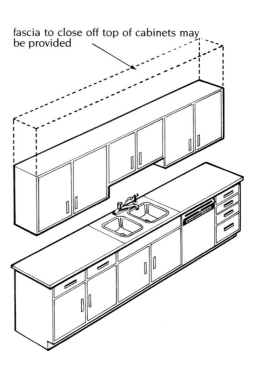

fascia to close off top of cabinets may
be provided

Automatic Dishwashers

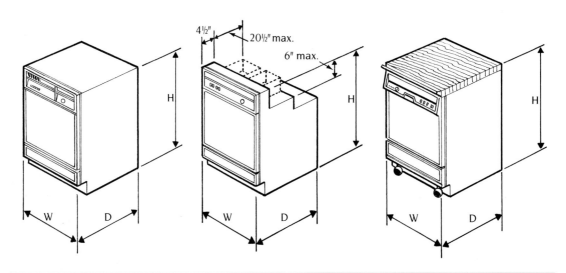

	Undercounter			Undersink			Mobile (with countertop)		
	Min.	Max.	Other	Min.	Max.	Other	Min.	Max.	Other
Width (in.)	23	24	23⅞	24	24¼	24	22½	27	24⅝
Depth (in.)	23¹¹⁄₁₆	26¼	25½	24	25½	25	23¹¹⁄₁₆	26½	25
Height (in.)	33½	34½	34⅛	34½	34½	34½	34⅛	39	36

RANGE CENTER
(cooking and serving)

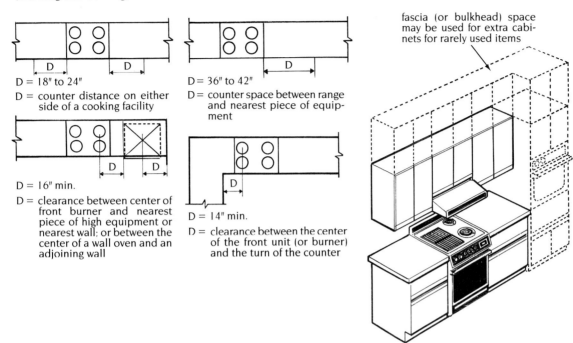

D = 18" to 24"

D = counter distance on either side of a cooking facility

D = 16" min.

D = clearance between center of front burner and nearest piece of high equipment or nearest wall; or between the center of a wall oven and an adjoining wall

D = 36" to 42"

D = counter space between range and nearest piece of equipment

D = 14" min.

D = clearance between the center of the front unit (or burner) and the turn of the counter

fascia (or bulkhead) space may be used for extra cabinets for rarely used items

The Range Center

The range center (for cooking and serving) provides storage for pots, pot holders, frying pans, roaster, cooking utensils, grease container, seasoning, canned goods, bread bin, breadboard, toaster, plate warmer, platters, serving dishes, and trays.

The Refrigerator Center

The refrigerator center (for receiving and food preparation) provides storage for mixer and mixing bowls; other utensils: sifter, grater, salad molds, cake and pie tins, occasional dishes, condiments, staples, canned goods, brooms, and miscellaneous items.

REFRIGERATOR CENTER
(receiving and food preparation)

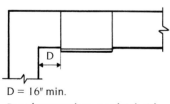

D = 16" min.

D = clearance between latch side of refrigerator door and turn of the counter

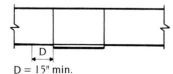

D = 15" min.

Provide room at latch side of refrigerator for loading and unloading

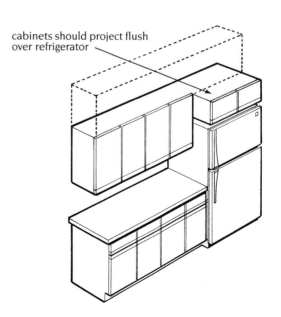

cabinets should project flush over refrigerator

Conventional Refrigerators

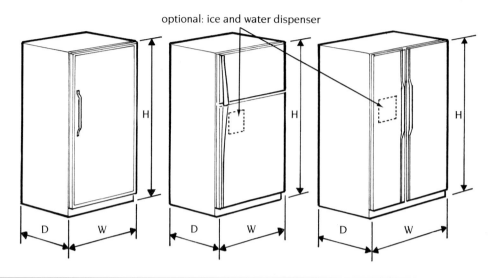

optional: ice and water dispenser

	Single Door		Top Freezer		Side-by-Side	
	Min.	Max.	Min.	Max.	Min.	Max.
Width (in.)	24	32¾	28	32¾	30½	35¾
Depth (in.)	26⁹⁄₁₆	31⅝	28¾	31⅝	29½	32⅞
Height (in.)	55½	63½	61	66	64	68⅞
Cubic ft.	9.5	14.0	11.8	22.4	18.5	25.6

Built-in Refrigerators

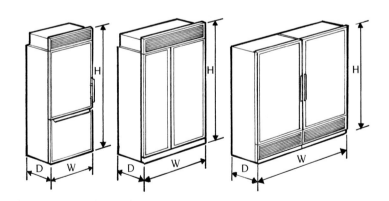

	Bottom Freezer		Side-by-Side		Combination
	Min.	Max.	Min.	Max.	Overall
Width (in.)	30	36	36	48	72
Depth (in.)	24	24	24	24	24
Height (in.)	84	84	84	84	73
Cubic ft.	19	23.6	24	32	42

Undercounter Refrigerators

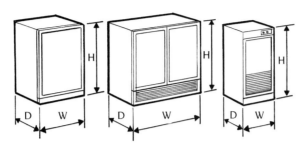

	Single Door	Side-by-Side	Automatic Ice-Cube Maker	
	Overall	Overall	Min.	Max.
Width (in.)	24	36	15	$17\frac{7}{8}$
Depth (in.)	$23\frac{3}{4}$	$23\frac{3}{4}$	$20\frac{3}{8}$	$23\frac{13}{16}$
Height (in.)	$34\frac{1}{2}$	$34\frac{1}{2}$	$33\frac{1}{8}$	$34\frac{13}{32}$
Cubic ft.	5.2	6.0	35 lb. of ice	

Freezers

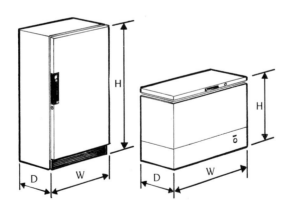

	Upright		Chest	
	Min.	Max.	Min.	Max.
Width (in.)	28	32	25	$69\frac{1}{2}$
Depth (in.)	$28\frac{7}{8}$	$30\frac{11}{16}$	$23\frac{1}{4}$	31
Height (in.)	$59\frac{1}{8}$	$70\frac{1}{8}$	$34\frac{11}{16}$	35
Cubic ft.	11.6	21.1	5.3	25.3

Childproofing Your Kitchen

- Store cleaning fluids, dangerous chemicals, and laundry detergents in wall cabinets.

- If possible, buy appliances with controls out of a child's reach.

- Avoid using throw rugs on waxed floors.

- Use strong rubber bands or special childproof latches to lock cabinets that contain dangerous utensils.

- Store your knives in a heavy drawer, which is difficult for a child to open, in an upper cabinet, or, at least, in a location where their blades are covered and they are out of a child's reach.

- Educate your child about hazards in the kitchen—few safeguards are as effective as education, supervision, and discipline.

- Consider establishing a child's cabinet—a place within easy reach where you can store snacks, plastic cups or plates, and other kitchen items a child might otherwise have to climb on top of a counter to find.

Kitchens for the Handicapped

Designing a kitchen for someone who is disabled requires attention to details. Nothing can be taken for granted. Of course, the extent of the modifications will depend on the disability of the person using the kitchen, as well as *how much* they will use it.

Altering a kitchen for use by a deaf person is largely a matter of replacing audible signals like buzzers with visual signals like flashing lights. A kitchen for use by someone who is blind requires more complex changes. Modifications include replacing control knobs on appliances with braille knobs, available from manufacturers; knurling or otherwise marking the knobs of cabinets with particularly dangerous contents; and using hard surfaces, which aid in sound detection. Gas ranges are recommended for the blind, because the cook can smell when they are turned on or are malfunctioning.

Making a kitchen accessible to a cook in a wheelchair is an extensive project. Space must be provided for turning the wheelchair. Heights of countertops and cabinets should be lower than the standard. Base cabinets should have pull-out vertical drawers, horizontal bins, and lazy Susans. Pull-out work shelves are handy. Upper cabinets are unusable by someone in a wheelchair, but frequently used utensils can be hung on pegboards or hooks. Oversize knobs are recommended for cabinets and drawers.

The space beneath the sink and food preparation areas should be left open, allowing a wheelchair to be pulled under the counter. It's a good idea to insulate the pipes to prevent burns to legs and feet. The sink should have a single-lever faucet mounted less than 21 inches from the edge of the counter; having 3 inches of space in front of the sink allows the cook to rest his or her elbows while washing dishes. A cooktop with separate wall ovens is easier for someone in a wheelchair to use. Controls for the cooktop should be located in front of the burners.

A hard, nonskid floor (brick or carpet) makes it easy to turn a wheelchair. Side-by-side refrigerators allow easy access to food—refrigerators with a top- or bottom-mounted freezer are difficult for someone in a wheelchair to use.

Measurements That Make Kitchens Wheelchair Friendly

Counter depth—21 to 24 inches

Counter heights—30 to 32 inches

Doors—32 inches minimum

Free space under work areas: 36 inches wide by 30 inches high by 24 inches deep

Maximum vertical reaches: overcounter, 44 inches; unimpeded, 48 inches

Passageways—36 inches wide

Sink depth—5 inches

Sink height—34 inches from floor

360-degree turns—require 64 inches minimum

Toe-kick space—7 inches deep by 10 inches high

Like all standard measurements, these are suggestions only. Some wheelchairs have a smaller turning radius, and some people are shorter or taller than others. The best approach is to design for the person who will be using the kitchen, sizing the space for the individual's needs.

Making Choices and a Budget

As you plan your new kitchen, use the blanks below to record the various components as you select them. Filling in these blanks will help you make decisions about what you will include in your new kitchen as well as serve as a record of these decisions. You'll want to list the type or style (i.e., a gas cooktop, an induction cooktop, a side-by-side refrigerator, and so forth) and the brand name with the model number. Then you will need to get even more specific as you complete the budget form.

Cabinets

Cabinets of _____ (laminate, wood, or a combination)
Brand name or cabinetmaker _____

Countertops

Countertops of _____ (material)
Brand name _____

Appliances

Cooktop _____ (type); brand name w/ model# _____
Microwave _____ (type); brand name w/ model# _____
Oven _____ (type); brand name w/ model# _____
Range _____ (type); brand name w/ model# _____

Refrigerator _____ (type); brand name w/ model# _____
Refrigerator/freezer _____ (type); brand name w/ model# _____
Freezer _____ (type); brand name w/ model# _____

Dishwasher _____ (type); brand name w/ model# _____
Garbage disposal _____ (type); brand name w/ model# _____
Trash compactor _____ (type); brand name w/ model# _____

Faucets _____ (type); brand name w/ model# _____
Sink _____ (type); brand name w/ model# _____
Water filter _____ (type); brand name w/ model# _____

Computer _____ (type); brand name w/ model# _____
TV _____ (type); brand name w/ model# _____
Radio/stereo _____ (type); brand name w/ model# _____

Lighting

Accent lighting _____ (type); brand name w/ model# _____
_____ (type); brand name w/ model# _____
Ambient lighting _____ (type); brand name w/ model# _____
_____ (type); brand name w/ model# _____
Task lighting _____ (type); brand name w/ model# _____
_____ (type); brand name w/ model# _____

Walls, Floors, and Ceilings

Ceiling _____ (type); brand name _____
Floor covering _____ (type); brand name _____
Wall covering _____ (type); brand name _____

Kitchen Budget Worksheet

Permits	$
Building	_____
Electric	_____
Plumbing	_____
Mechanical	_____

Removal of construction trash

Dumpster	_____
Dump fee	_____
Trash hauling	_____

Labor

Demolition	_____
Carpentry	_____
Rough	_____
Finish	_____
Hanging of cabinets	_____
Wiring	
Rough	_____
Finish	_____
Plumbing	
Rough	_____
Finish	_____
Drywalling	
Hanging	_____
Taping and sealing	_____
Sheet-metal work	
Ducting for hood	_____
Relocating floor and wall heat ducts	_____
Counters	_____
Floors	_____
Finish work	
Painting	_____
Wallpapering	_____

Materials*

Appliances	
Compactor	_____
Cooktop	_____
Dishwasher	_____
Freezer	_____

Materials (continued)

Garbage disposal	_____
Grill	_____
Microwave	_____
Oven	_____
Range hood	_____
Refrigerator	_____
Warming oven	_____
Cabinets	_____
Countertops	_____
Door(s)	_____
Faucet(s)	_____
Floor	_____
Sink(s)	_____
Windows	_____

Miscellaneous items

Carpentry	
2 × 4s	
Headers	_____
Miscellaneous lumber	_____
Nails	_____
Insulation	_____
Electric supplies	
Wire	_____
Boxes	_____
Connectors	_____
Plugs, switches, and dimmers	_____
Miscellaneous supplies	_____
Lighting fixtures	
Recessed	_____
Undercabinet	_____
Surface-mounted	_____
Plumbing	
Pipe	_____
Connectors and fittings	_____
Drywall	
Tape, joint compound, and corner fittings	_____

*Include tax and delivery charges.

Miscellaneous items (continued)
    Finishing materials   Window
       Moldings   _____   treatment(s)   _____
       Paint   _____
       Wallpaper   _____
       Special
          backsplash   _____   *Design fee*   _____

Kitchen Remodeling Legalities

Why should you have a written contract for your kitchen remodeling? First, and probably most importantly, written agreements don't suffer from memory loss. People, all people, tend to forget things over time, and writing agreements down helps to preserve the facts of the agreement. Next, writing down the agreement may help you to anticipate problems with the project itself, such as having overlooked one or more major items. If you invest some time in its preparation, writing down the agreement may avoid some of the common ambiguities that give rise to disputes, such as who is responsible for locating various items or doing the cleanup work. One of the most common disputes centers around the delayed completion of the project, with the homeowner claiming that he or she told the contractor that the kitchen had to be finished for a certain event and the contractor, in turn, denying any knowledge of any performance requirements.

Accordingly, your contract should specify both a starting and ending date for the remodeling work. This (generally) forces the contractor to plan his or her work a little more carefully and, when tied to a penalty clause, may cause the contractor to be more diligent in the remodeling work. Be wary of preprinted form contracts that just specify a starting date; you have the right to know when the project will be completed.

By the same token, try to consider the realities of your project. Many times, the homeowner (or the architect) does not allow for out-of-stock items or time delays when items have to be custom-made. While it is usually the contractor's responsibility to determine the availability of materials, if your custom-made, Italian marble countertop falls off the boat, there's not much the contractor can do about it!

Your contract should also specify the grade and brand (if possible) of the materials to be used, in addition to the total price. Merely specifying the color, finish, and size leaves much to the imagination of your contractor, who, if working under a fixed-price agreement, has built-in incentives to cut corners. This is not to suggest that every builder will use the cheapest materials around, but you should consider the possibilities!

Some sample clauses and the reasons for their inclusion in a contract are given on pages 142-43. *Please* remember two very important points:

1. These are sample clauses only, provided as a guideline for you. It is impossible to anticipate every contingency in every situation. Thus, you should, after you have drafted the

contract and *before* your contractor and you sign it, have it reviewed by an attorney familiar with construction law. Your local bar association can arrange for you to meet, for a minimal fee, with a lawyer who will discuss the contract with you and suggest any necessary changes.

2. There is no such thing as a perfect contract or one that meets everyone's needs. Thus, feel free to modify the sample clauses to meet your own requirements and expectations.

Sample Clauses in a Kitchen Remodeling Contract

> This agreement is entered into on this ____ day of _____, 19__ by and between _____
> known in this agreement as "Owner" and _____, known in this agreement as "Contractor."

The purpose of this clause is to identify the parties to the contract. It is important that both the contractor and you give your full and complete legal names.

> Owner and Contractor agree that this agreement shall govern the work to be performed in the remodeling and/or reconstruction of the kitchen of Owner's residence located at |GIVE ADDRESS| and as is more clearly set forth in those certain drawings and specifications prepared by |NAME OF ARCHITECT OR KITCHEN DESIGNER| and dated _____, 19__, true and correct copies of which are attached to this agreement.

Don't even think of remodeling your kitchen without drawings and specifications! Probably more disputes arise because of disagreements over the scope of the work than for any other reason. It is absolutely essential that both the contractor and you agree, at least in the beginning, as to what you expect the contractor to do and what services the contractor expects to perform. Remember, the contractor prepared his or her bid based on an expectation of performing a certain level of work and materials.

> Owner agrees that Contractor shall be paid the total sum of $____ as follows, subject to any adjustments which may be made between the parties or as a result of Contractor's failure to perform in accordance with the terms of this agreement:
>
> $_____ upon the signing of this agreement;
>
> $_____ on completion of Contractor's work; and
>
> $_____ upon the expiration of |NUMBER| days.

This clause has multiple purposes. First, it establishes the maximum price for the work as bid and recognizes that the price may ultimately change, but only in accordance with the agreement itself. Second, the contract establishes a phased payment schedule, so that the contractor has to perform to get paid; the theory is to not allow the contractor to get ahead of you—better you should owe him or her. Many states limit the amount of deposit that a contractor can demand; this information is readily obtainable from the contractor's licensing agency in your state. For a simple remodeling job the above schedule may be appropriate; more complex projects may require more frequent payments. Finally, this schedule provides for a "holdback" of funds until the time for filing mechanic's liens has run; this will usually be between 30 and 90 days. The reason for this provision is to allow you to determine that all subcontractors have, in fact, been paid by the general contractor. A competent lawyer can explain the various rules concerning mechanic's liens in your state.

> Contractor agrees that work shall begin not later than _____, 19__, and be completed not later than _____, 19__. In the event that Contractor fails to complete the work by the latter date, then Contractor agrees to pay Owner the sum of $____ per day for each day of delay. This provision may only be modified or waived by the written agreement of Owner.

Contractors do not like this provision, but they will sign it! Inclusion of this provision forces a contractor to plan the work flow more carefully, usually to the benefit of both the contractor and you!

> Contractor agrees that no extras shall be paid for unless Owner's agreement, in writing, is first obtained.

The infamous change orders! Be sure that each deviation from the plans and specifications is documented and that you know the full cost of each change. It is very easy to go over budget by "making a change here and there"—each change can affect the completion date of the project.

> Contractor warrants that all work and materials shall be warranted for a period of one year from the date of completion of the project, notwithstanding any manufacturer's warranties. Contractor agrees that he shall be responsible for and shall repair all damage to the premises, landscaping, and personal property and shall hold Owner harmless for any liability therefore. Contractor further warrants that all work shall be performed in a workmanlike manner, in accordance with the highest standards of the industry, and that at all times during the term of this agreement, Contractor shall be in full compliance with all licensing, insurance, and other relevant laws and regulations.

This clause is to obligate the contractor to repair any problems that arise after completion of the work. Most contractors would rely on you to get a defective dishwasher or disposal repaired; this provision puts the responsibility on the contractor. The clause also requires the contractor to maintain any necessary licenses or insurance. But don't take the contractor's word for it; ask to see the originals of licenses and insurance policies.

> Owner and Contractor agree that in the event of a dispute concerning the subject matter of this agreement, said dispute shall be resolved by an arbitration conducted in accordance with and under the auspices of the American Arbitration Association.

Arbitration is one way to handle disputes. The advantages are that it is faster, and many arbitrators are familiar with construction law. While it is sometimes cheaper than going to court, a complex arbitration can be as costly as a court trial and will require the skills of a competent attorney. This clause is optional and should be discussed with an experienced attorney.

> The parties agree that this agreement was signed on date first written above at |ADDRESS|

Followed by signature lines, this provision establishes that the agreement was signed on the specified date and also where it was signed, for purposes of determining the proper court in which to file a lawsuit, if that ultimately becomes necessary.

You might also include other clauses regarding when and where deliveries are to be made, when you will consider the project completed, and where payment is to be made if the contractor is providing you with financing. Which clauses you will include will depend upon your own particular situation.

Above all, remember that communication with your contractor will solve most, if not all of the problems that might arise, and that time spent discussing the problem will usually make the problem disappear.

Helpful Addresses

Organizations

American Institute of Architects (AIA)
1735 New York Ave. NW
Washington, D.C. 20006

American Home Lighting Institute
230 N. Michigan Ave.
Chicago, IL 60601

American Society of Interior Designers
1430 Broadway
New York, NY 10018

Association of Home Appliance
    Manufacturers (AHAM)
20 N. Wacker Dr.
Chicago, IL 60606

Illuminating Engineering Society
345 E. 47th St.
New York, NY 10017

National Kitchen and Bath Association
124 Main St.
Hackettstown, NJ 07840

Manufacturers
Air-to-Air Heat Exchangers

Mitsubishi Electric Sales America, Inc.
P. O. Box 6007
5757 Plaza Dr.
Cypress, CA 90630-0007

Appliances

Amana Refrigeration, Inc.
Amana, IA 52204

Andi-Co Appliances Inc. (AEG)
Suite 301
2100 N. Central Rd.
Fort Lee, NJ 07024

Bacun, Inc. (Fasar)
2801 Burton Ave.
Burbank, CA 91504

Black & Decker (U.S.) Inc.
Housewares Group
1285 Boston Ave.
Bridgeport, CT 06610

Braun Inc.
66 Broadway, Rte. 1
Lynnfield, MA 01940

Brookstone Co.
Vose Farm Rd.
Peterborough, NH 03458

Caloric Corp.
403 N. Main St.
Topton, PA 19562-1499

Casablanca Fan Co.
P. O. Box 424
City of Industry, CA 91747

Coalbrookdale/Aga
R.F.D. 1
Box 477
Stowe, VT 05672

Cuisinarts, Inc.
411 W. Putnam Ave.
Greenwich, CT 06830

Frigidaire Co.
3555 S. Kettering Blvd.
P. O. Box WC4900
Dayton, OH 45449

Gaggenau USA Corp.
5 Commonwealth Ave.
Woburn, MA 01801

General Electric Co.
Campus Center, Suite 106
120 Gibraltar Rd.
Horsham, PA 19044

Glynwed International (Aga)
R.F.D. 1
Box 477
Stowe, VT 05672

Hobart Corp.
KitchenAid Division
711 World Headquarters Ave.
Troy, OH 45374

Hotpoint (General Electric)
Appliance Park
Louisville, KY 40225

Hunter Fan Co.
2500 Frisco Ave.
Memphis, TN 38114

Jenn-Air Co.
3035 N. Shadeland Ave.
Indianapolis, IN 46226

Litton Microwave Cooking Products
1405 Xenium La.
P. O. Box 9461
Minneapolis, MN 55441

Magic Chef, Inc.
740 King Edward Ave.
Cleveland, TN 37311

Miele Appliances, Inc.
12F Worlds Fair Dr.
Somerset, NJ 08873

Modern Maid
403 N. Main St.
Topton, PA 19562-1499

North American Philips Corp.
100 E. 42nd St.
New York, NY 10017

NuTone Division Scoville, Inc.
Madison and Red Banks Rd.
Cincinnati, OH 45227

Oster Corp.
5055 N Lydell St.
Milwaukee, WI 53217

Rival Manufacturing Co.
36 and Vennington St.
Kansas City, MO 64129

Russell Hobbs
P. O. Box 241
Pompton Plains, NJ 07444

Sanyo Electric Inc.
200 Riser Rd.
Little Ferry, NJ 07643

Sears, Roebuck & Co.
Sears Tower
Chicago, IL 60684

Sharp Electronics Corp.
10 Sharp Plaza
P. O. Box 588
Paramus, NJ 07652

Solinger and Associates (Garland)
4 S. Walker
P. O. Box 196
Clarendon Hills, IL 60514

Sub-Zero Freezer Co., Inc.
P. O. Box 4130
Madison, WI 53711

Sunbeam Appliance Co.
2900 S. 21st Ave.
Broadview, IL 60153

Taylor & Ng.
2700 Maxwell Way
P. O. Box 8888
Fairfield, CA 94533

Thermador/Waste King
Division of Ni Industries, Inc.
5119 District Blvd.
Los Angeles, CA 90040

Toastmaster Inc.
1801 N. Stadium Blvd.
Columbia, MI 65202

Toshiba America, Inc.
82 Totowa Rd.
Wayne, NJ 07470

Traulsen & Company, Inc.
114-02 15th Ave.
College Point, NY 11356

Waring Products Division
Dynamics Corp. of America
Rte. 44
New Hartford, CT 06057

Whirlpool Corp.
2000 US 33 North
Benton Harbor, MI 49022

White-Westinghouse Appliance Co.
930 Fort Duquesne Blvd.
Pittsburgh, PA 15222

Wolf Range Co.
19600 S. Alameda St.
P. O. Box 7050
Compton, CA 90224

Cabinets

Allmilmö
70 Clinton Rd.
P. O. Box 629
Fairfield, NJ 07006

Alno Kitchen Cabinets
109 Wattoo Creek Dr.
Suite 4B
Charleston, SC 29411

Heritage Custom Kitchens, Inc.
215 Diller Ave.
New Holland, PA 17557

Kitchens from Germany, Ltd.
6900 Peachtree Industrial Blvd.
Suite F
Narcross, GA 30071

Merillat Industries, Inc.
2075 W. Beecher Rd.
Adrian, MI 49221

Millbrook Custom Kitchens
P. O. Box 21
Rte. 20
Nassau, NY 12123

Poggenpohl USA Corp.
6 Pearl Ct.
Allendale, NJ 07401

Quakermaid
Rte. 61
Leesport, PA 19533

Rational Cabinets USA
1560 W. Winton Ave.
Hayward, CA 94545

St. Charles Manufacturing Co.
St. Charles, IL 60174

Scheirich Cabinetry
250 Ottawa Ave.
P. O. Box 37120
Louisville, KY 40233-7120

Style Craft Kitchens
Box 458
Blue Ball, PA 17506

Triangle Pacific Corp.
16803 Dallas Pkwy.
P.O. Box 660100
Dallas, TX 75266-0110

Wood-Mode Cabinetry
Snyder Co.
Kreamer, PA 17833

Yorktowne Cabinets
P. O. Box 231
Red Lion, PA 17356

Cabinet Hardware

Amerock Corp.
4000 Auburn St.
P. O. Box 7018
Rockford, IL 61101

Feeny Manufacturing Co.
P. O. Box 191
Muncie, IN 47305

Grass America, Inc.
P. O. Box 1019
1377 S. Park. Dr.
Kernersville, NC 27284

Hafele America Co.
P. O. Box 1590
High Point, NC 27261

Corian

E. I. Du Pont De Nemours & Co.
1007 Marketing St.
Wilmington, DE 19898

Entertainment Equipment

Panasonic Co.
One Panasonic Way
Secaucus, NJ 07094

Sony Corp. of America
Sony Dr.
Park Ridge, NJ 07656

Yamaha International Corp.
6600 Orange Thorpe Ave.
Buena Park. CA 90620

Zenith Electronics Corp.
1000 Milwaukee Ave.
Glenview, IL 60025

Floor Coverings (see also "Tile" on pp. 146-47)

Armstrong World Industries, Inc.
P. O. Box 3001
Lancaster, PA 17604

Azrock Industries Inc.
Azrock Floor Products Division
P. O. Box 34030
San Antonio, TX 78265

Bruce Hardwood Floors
16803 Dallas Pkwy.
Dallas, TX 75248

Hartco, Inc.
P. O. Box 1001
Oneida, TN 37841

Memphis Hardwood Flooring Co.
P. O. Box 7253
1551 Thomas St.
Memphis TN 38107

Missouri Hardwood Flooring Co.
P. O. Box 117
Birch Tree, MO 65438

National Oak Flooring Manufacturers'
Association
8 N. Third St.
Suite 810, Sterick Bldg.
Memphis, TN 38103

Natural Vinyl Floor Co., Inc.
P. O. Box 1302
Florence, AL 35631

Nora Flooring
4201 Wilson Ave.
Madison, IN 47250

Parkett Flooring
P. O. Box 264-800
Landex Plaza
Parsippany. NJ 07054

Triangle Pacific Corp.
16803 Dallas Pkwy.
P. O. Box 660100
Dallas, TX 75266-0110

Kit Cabinets

Cabinetmaster
P. O. Box 6536
Colorado Springs, CO 80934

Knockdown Cabinets

American Marketing and Management, Inc.
(Distributor of Euroline)
194 Hackensack St.
Wood-Ridge, NJ 07075

Famco Distributor, Inc.
(Distributor of Contempo Starter Pack
Cabinets)
166 58th St.
Brooklyn, NY 11232

Laminates

Consoweld Corp.
700 Durabeauty La.
Wisconsin Rapids, WI 54494

Formica Corp.
Cyanamid Division
1 Cyanamid Plaza
Wayne, NJ 07470

Laminart, Inc.
1330 Mark St.
Elk Grove Village, IL 60007

Laminates Unlimited, Inc.
5500 E. Lombard St.
Baltimore, MD 21224

Nevamar Corp.
8339 Telegraph Rd.
Odenton, MD 21113

Pioneer Plastics
Division of LOF Plastics, Inc.
Pionite Rd.
Auburn, ME 04210

Suncraft Moldings, Inc.
650 SE Ninth St.
Bend, OR 97702

Laminates (continued)

Westinghouse Electric Co.
P. O. Box 248
Hampton, SC 29924

Wilsonart Information Center
Ralph Wilson Plastics Corp.
600 General Bruce Dr.
Temple, TX 76501

Lighting

Aladdin Industries, Inc.
P. O. Box 100255
Nashville, TN 37210

Duro-Test Corp.
2321 Kennedy Blvd.
North Bergen, NJ 07047

Dynascan Corp.
6460 W. Cortland St.
Chicago, IL 60635

General Electric Co.
Campus Center, Suite 106
120 Gibraltar Rd.
Horsham, PA 19044

GTE Products Corp.
Sylvania Lighting Center
100 Endicott St.
Danvers, MA 01923

Halo Lighting
Division of Cooper Industries
400 Busse Rd.
Elk Grove Village, IL 60007

Lightolier Genlyte, Inc.
346 Claremont Ave.
Jersey City, NJ 07305

Lutron Electronics Co., Inc.
Suter Rd.
Coopersburg, PA 18036

Moore Lambert Industries, Inc.
2237 Colby Ave.
P. O. Box 64428
Los Angeles, CA 90064

North American Philips Lighting Corp.
Bank St.
Hightstown, NJ 08520

Peerless Electric Co.
747 Bancroft Way
Berkeley, CA 94710

Progress Lighting
Subsidiary of Walter Kidde and Co., Inc.
G St. and Erie Ave.
Philadelphia, PA 19134

R E C Specialties, Inc.
530 Constitution Ave.
Camarillo, CA 93010

Sears, Roebuck & Co.
Sears Tower
Chicago, IL 60684

Thomas Industries Inc.
207 E. Broadway
Louisville, KY 40232

Marble, Stone, and Brick

Bergen Bluestone Co., Inc.
404 Rte. 17 N.
P. O. Box 67
Paramus, NJ 07652

Boren Clay Products Co.
P. O. Box 368
Pleasant Garden, NC 27313

Cold Spring Granite Co.
202 S. Third Ave.
Cold Spring, MN 56320

Endicott Clay Products Co.
Endicott, NE 68350

Marble Technics Ltd.
150 E. 58th St.
New York, NY 10155

Phillipsburg Marble Co.,Inc.
River Rd.
Phillipsburg, NJ 08865

Sinks and/or Faucets

Abbaka
435 23rd St.
San Francisco, CA 94107

American-Standard
555 River Rd.
Piscataway, NJ 08854

Artistic Brass
A Division of Norris Industries
3136 E. 11th St.
Los Angeles, CA 90023

Blanco-Globass Distribution Center
P. O. Box 24190
Tampa, FL 33623

Chicago Faucets
2100 S. Nuclear Dr.
Des Plaines, IL 60018

Delta Faucet Co.
Division of Masco Corp. of Indiana
55 E. 111th St.
P. O. Box 40980
Indianapolis, IN 46280

Eljer Plumbingware
Three Gateway Center
Pittsburgh, PA 15222

Elkay Manufacturing Co.
2222 Camden Ct.
Oak Brook, IL 60521

Franke, Inc.
Kitchens System Division
212 Church Rd.
North Wales, PA 19454

Grohe America, Inc.
900 Lively Blvd.
Wood Dale, IL 60191

Harden Industries
P. O. Box 5991
13813 S. Main St.
Los Angeles, CA 90059

Jensen-Thorsen Corp.
2443 Bragh Cr.
Broadview, IL 60153

Kohler Co.
444 Highland Dr.
Kohler, WI 53044

Luwa Corp.
Builder Products Division
P. O. Box 16348
Charlotte, NC 28297-6348

Moen Group
Stanadyne, Inc.
377 Woodland Ave.
P. O. Box 4007
Elyria, OH 44036

Price Pfister, Inc.
13500 Paxton St.
P. O. Box 637
Pacoima, CA 91331-0637

Revere Sink Corp.
P. O. Box N-1157
New Bedford, MA 02746

Santile International Corp.
W. Loop Business Park
1201 W. Loop North, Suite 170
Houston, TX 77055

Sears, Roebuck & Co.
Sears Tower
Chicago, IL 60684

Sloan Valve Co.
10500 Seymour Ave.
Franklin Park, IL 60131

Stainless Steel Sinks, Inc.
300 Fay Ave.
P. O. Box 296
Addison, IL 60101

Sterling Faucet Co.
P. O. Box 798
Morgantown, WV 26505

UNR Home Products
P. O. Box 429
Paris, IL 61944

Vance Industries, Inc.
7401 W. Wilson Ave.
Chicago, IL 60656

Tankless, Point-of-Use Water Heaters

Chronomite Laboratories, Inc.
21011 S. Figueroa St.
Carson, CA 90745

Thermar Corp.
Melrose Square
Greenwich, CT 06830

Tile

American Olean Tile Co.
1000 Cannon Ave.
P. O. Box 271
Lansdale, PA 19446-0271

The Briare Co., Inc.
51 Tec St.
Hicksville, NY 11801

Country Floors
300 E. 61st St.
New York, NY 10021

Elon Inc.
150 E. 58th St.
New York, NY 10155

Endicott Clay Products Co.,
Endicott, NE 68350

International Tile and Supply Corp.
1288 S. La Brea Ave.
Los Angeles, CA 90019

Italian Tile Center
499 Park Ave.
New York, NY 10022

Kentile Floors, Inc.
58 Second Ave.
Brooklyn, NY 11215

Metropolitan Industries, Inc.
P. O. Box 9240
Canton, OH 44711

Mid-State Tile Co.
P. O. Box 1777
Lexington, NC 27292

Monarch Tile Manufacturing, Inc.
1 E. Twohit St.
P. O. Box 2041
San Angelo, TX 76902

Moravian Pottery & Tile Works
130 Swamp Rd.
Doylestown, PA 18901

Rico Tile Co.
17 E. Jerco Tpke.
Huntington Station, NY 11746

Ro-Tile Inc.
1625 S. Stockton St.
P. O. Box 410
Lodi, CA 95240

San Francisco Tile Co.
430 9th St.
San Francisco, CA 94103

Sikes Corp.
Division of Florida Tile
P. O. Box 447
Lakeland, FL 33802

Summitville Tiles Inc.
P. O. Box 73
Summitville, OH 43962

Villeroy & Boch
P. O. Box 103
Interstate 80 at New Maple Ave.
Pinebrook, NJ 07058

Walker and Zanger (West Coast Limited)
1832 S. Brand Blvd.
Glendale, CA 91204

Wenczel Tile Co.
P. O. Box 5308
Trenton, NJ 08638

Wall Coverings

Abitibi-Price Corp.
3250 W. Big Beaver
Building Products Group
Troy, MI 48084

American Olean Tile Co.
1000 Cannon Ave.
P. O. Box 271
Lansdale, PA 19446

Bangkok Industries, Inc.
4562 Worth St.
Philadelphia, PA 19124

Columbus Coated Fabrics
1280 N. Grant Ave.
Columbus, OH 43216

Forms & Surfaces, Inc.
P. O. Box 5215
Santa Barbara, CA 93150

Georgia-Pacific Corp.
P. O. Box 105605
133 Peachtree Street NE
Atlanta, GA 30348-5605

Gold Bond Building Products
2001 Rexford Rd.
Charlotte, NC 28211

Hastings Pavement Co., Inc.
370 Commercial St.
Freeport, NY 11520

Motif Designs
20 Jones St.
New Rochelle, NY 10801

Ralph Wilson Plastics Corp.
600 General Bruce Dr.
Temple TX 76501

Roseburg Forest Products Co.
P. O. Box 1088
Roseburg, OR 97470

Seacrest Handprints
2 Neil Ct.
Oceanside, NY 11572

USG Corporation
101 S. Wacker Dr.
Chicago, IL 60606

Weyerhaeuser Company
Paneling Division Headquarters
201 Dexter St.
P. O. Box 1188
Chesapeake, VA 23320

Windows

Andersen Corp.
Bayport, MN 55003

Caradco Corp.
201 Evans Dr.
P. O. Box 920
Rantoul, IL 61866

CertainTeed Corp.
P. O. Box 860
Valley Forge, PA 19482

Kirsh Co.
309 N. Prospect St.
Sturgis, MI 49091

Marvin Windows Co.
P. O. Box 100
Warroad, MN 56763

Norco Windows, Inc.
P. O. Box 309
U.S. Highway #8
Hawkins, WI 54530

Paeco Industries, Inc.
One Executive Dr.
P. O. Box 968
Toms River, NJ 08753

Plasteco, Inc.
P. O. Box 24158
Houston, TX 77229-4158

Rolscreen Co./Pella
102 Main St.
Pella, IA 50219

Tub-Master Corp.
413 Virginia Dr.
Orlando, FL 32803

Velux-America, Inc.
450 Old Brickyard Rd.
P. O. Box 3208
Greenwood, SC 29648

Webb Manufacturing, Inc.
1209 Maple Ave.
P. O. Box 707
Conneaut, OH 44030

CREDITS

Notes
A New Version of the Hearth

"A New Version of the Hearth" by Jeremiah Eck. "The Too Small Kitchen" and "Lighting Strategies" by Michael Stoner. "Questions to Answer before You Begin," "Sizing Up Your Present Kitchen," and "Planning a Smart Kitchen," by Beverly Wilson. "A Balanced Budget" by Wilson and Stoner. "A Remodeling Time Line" by Wilson.

Cabinets and Countertops

"Cabinets and Countertops," "Types of Cabinets," "Counter Points," and "Sinks and Faucets" by Wilson. "Assemble-Yourself Cabinets" by Catherine M. Poole. "Behind the Cabinet Door" and "Islands and Peninsulas" by Stoner. "The New Laminates" by Marguerite Smolen. "Pure Water on Tap" by Craig Canine.

Appliances

"What's Cooking?" "The Big Chill," and "Cleaning Up" by Wilson. "Breathing Easier in the Kitchen" by Michael Lafavore. "Pots and Pans," "Energy-Efficient Refrigerators," and "Small Appliances" by Stoner.

Walls, Floors, and Ceilings

By Wilson and Stoner.

Gallery: A Tour of Fine Kitchens

By Stoner except for the following: "A Kitchen for Natural Foods Gourmets" and "A Respect for Tradition" by Smolen. "Opening Up the Galley" by Canine. "A Compact Kitchen" by Lafavore.

Workbook: The Basics of Kitchen Design

"How to Use an Architectural Scale" and "Kitchen Budget Worksheet" by Wilson. "Childproofing Your Kitchen" by Stoner. "Kitchen Remodeling Legalities" by Sidney J. Hymes.

Photography Credits

Below are the credits for each photograph. The first name is that of the photographer, followed by the names of the designer, craftsman, or photo stylist, when applicable.

Title page: Mitchell T. Mandel; photo styling. J. C. Vera

P. vi: Mitchell T. Mandel; design, Thomas M. Hemphill, Case Design/Remodeling Inc., 5135 MacArthur Blvd. NW, Washington, DC 20016

P. 1: J. Michael Kanouff; design, Sally S. Tantau, P. O. Box 302, St. Helena, CA 94574; general contractor, Russ Burr, 1551 Oak Ave., St. Helena, CA 94574

Pp. 2-3: Mitchell T. Mandel; design, Dr. and Mrs. John Cavallo

P. 4 Mitchell T. Mandel; design, Steve Myrwang of Myrwang Associates Architects, 311½ Occidental Ave. S., Suite 300, Seattle, WA 98104

P. 5: J. Michael Kanouff; design, Sid Del Leach, 288 Butterfield Rd., San Anselmo, CA 94960

P. 6: courtesy of Poggenpohl USA Corp.

P. 7: courtesy of Armstrong World Industries, Inc.

P. 8: T. L. Gettings; craftsman, Richard C. Weinsteiger

P. 9: Mitchell T. Mandel; design, Steve Myrwang

P. 10: Mitchell T. Mandel

P. 11 (upper): Mark Lenny; photo styling, Renee R. Keith; design, Robert L. Wieland and Iris Konia

P. 11 (lower): photo courtesy of LA Associates, 317 NE 24th St., Miami, FL 33137

P. 14: J. Michael Kanouff; design, Sid Del Leach

P. 15: J. Michael Kanouff; design, Daniel Merkle, Sunworks, Inc., Portland, Oreg.

P. 18: J. Michael Kanouff; design, Steve Doriss, IO Design, P. O. Box 245, Albion, CA 95410

P. 19: J. Michael Kanouff; design, Sears Barrett, AIA

P. 25: J. Michael Kanouff; design, Beverly Wilson, 570 Woodmont Ave., Berkeley. CA 94708; architecture, Ron Bogley, 2124 Ward St., Berkeley, CA 94705

Pp. 26-27: Mitchell T. Mandel; design, Paul Pietz, AIA, Pietz & Michal Architects, 20 West St., Keene, NH 03431

P. 29: courtesy of Allmilmö

P. 30: J. Michael Kanouff; design, Sears Barrett, AIA

P. 31: Mark Lenny; design, Jack Schemm

P. 32 (upper): J. Michael Kanouff; craftsman, Steve Doriss

P. 32 (lower): John Hamel; glasswork, Earl McFarland; cabinetry, Roger Gray

P. 33: J. Michael Kanouff; design, Sid Del Leach

P. 34: photo courtesy of American Marketing and Management, Inc.

P. 35: Mark Lenny

P. 36 (left): Mitchell T. Mandel; photo styling, J. C. Vera

P. 36 (right): Mark Lenny

P. 37: Mark Lenny; photo styling, Renee R. Keith

P. 38 (left): Mitchell T. Mandel; glasswork, Roberta Katz; cabinetry design, Robert Maria

P. 38 (right): J. Michael Kanouff; cabinetry design, John Vugrin

P. 39 (upper left): Mitchell T. Mandel; photo styling, J. C. Vera

P. 39 (upper right): Margaret Lydic Balitas

P. 39 (lower): J. Michael Kanouff; design, Beverly Wilson

P. 40 (upper): Mitchell T. Mandel; photo styling, Kathy Boucher

P. 40 (lower) and p. 41 (upper): Mitchell T. Mandel

P. 41 (lower): John Hamel

P. 42: photo courtesy of Formica Corp.; design, Mark Simon

P. 43: photo courtesy of Wilsonart

P. 44: photo courtesy of Quakermaid

P. 45: photo courtesy of Formica Corp.

Credits for "Gallery: A Tour of Fine Kitchens"

"A Living-Hall Kitchen" (pp. 82-83): **house and kitchen design** by Jeremiah Eck, Architect, AIA, 129 Portland St., Boston, MA 02114; **cabinets** by Wood-Mode; **ceiling fan** by Hunter; **cooktop** by Jenn-Air; **countertop** is Formica laminate with cherry trim; **dishwasher** by GE; **floor covering** is Mexican tile; **microwave** by GE; **oven** (convection/conventional combination) by Jenn-Air; **refrigerator** by Sub-Zero; **stereo** by Zenith; **TV** by Sony.

"A Kitchen of Color" (pp. 84-85): **kitchen design** by James Kershaw, CKD.

The Hammer & Nail, 232 Madison Ave., Wyckoff, NJ 07481; **architecture** by Heidi Kleinman, Architect, 107 Demarest Rd., Bloomingdale, NJ 07403; **cabinets** by The Hammer & Nail in Formica 857, Fiesta Bisque; **cooktop** by Thermador; **countertop** is Formica laminate; **dishwasher** by KitchenAid; **faucet** by Franke; **floor covering** is Ceramiche Folivesi, Wayne Tile Co., 1459 Rte. 23, Wayne, NJ 07470; **microwave** by Amana; **ovens and refrigerator** by GE; **sinks** (kitchen) by Franke and (bar) Elkay.

"A Team Approach to Kitchen Design" (pp. 86-87): **kitchen design** by Janine J. Newlin, CKD, ISID, J. J. Newlin Interiors, 42 Whippoorwill Road, Chappaqua, NY 10514; **addition to house** designed by John Eide, AIA, 517 King St., Chappaqua, NY 10514; **additional design in kitchen** by Lee Kowalski, CKD, Kitchen Originals, 202 Field Point Rd., Greenwich, CT 06830; **cabinets** designed by Lee Kowalski and built by Heritage Custom Kitchens; **contractor** was Carbut Building Corp., 46 Woodland Rd., Mount Kisco, NY 10549; **cooktop** by Thermador; **countertop** is Corian by Du Pont; **dishwasher** by GE; **faucets** by Moen; **freezer** by Sub-Zero; **grill** by Jenn-Air; **oven** (microwave/conventional combination) by Thermador; **refrigerator** by Sub-Zero; **sink** by Elkay; **tile** is American Olean, Gardenia Brite and Matte series with design painted and overglazed by Phyllis Traynor, Scotts Corners, Pound Ridge, NY 10576; **trash compactor** by Thermador.

"A European Country Kitchen" (pp. 88-89): **kitchen design** by Dr. and Mrs. John Cavallo; **cabinets** custom-made by Tom Dietrich; **countertops** are butcher block and marble slabs, which are from Phillipsburg Marble, with Formica around the sink; **dishwasher** by Waste King; **floor covering** of marble tiles from Phillipsburg Marble; **commercial range** (60 inch) by Garland; **refrigerator** by Sub-Zero; **sink and faucets** by Elkay.

"A Kitchen for Natural Foods Gourmets" (pp. 90-91): **kitchen design** by David Goldbeck, P.O. Box 87, Woodstock, NY 12498; **builder** was Stephen Robin Associates, P.O. Box 283, Woodstock, NY 12498; **air cleaner** by Air Conditioning Engineers, P.O. Box 616, Decatur, IL 62525; **blender** by Oster; **chrome plating** by Chandler Royce, 185 E. 122nd St., New York, NY 10035; **clear red oak flooring** by Missouri Hardwood Flooring Co. and National Oak Flooring Manufacturers' Assn.; **clock** by Bulova Clocks, Bulova Park, Flushing, NY 11370; **computers and software** by Kaypro Corp., P.O. Box 9, Del Mar, CA 92014 and by P & B Computer Services, Inc., 13701 NE BelRed Rd., Bellevue, WA 98005 and Software Toolworks, 15233 Ventura Blvd.,

"Natural Foods Gourmets" (continued)

Sherman Oaks, CA 91403; **cooktop** by Modern Maid; **cookware** by Primex International Trading Corp., 41 Madison Ave., New York, NY 10010; **dehydrator heater-blower** by NutriFlow, 810 NW 11th St., Portland, OR 97209; **digital refrigerator thermometer, Energy Teller, faucet water miser, oven thermometer, silicone spray, and undercabinet jar opener** from Brookstone; **dimmers and fan speed control** by Lutron Electronics Co., Inc.; **dishwasher, ergonomic chair, and fire extinguisher** by Sears, Roebuck and Co.; **Dustbuster and Toast-R-Oven** by Black & Decker; **etched-glass doors** by Gene Mallaid, 11½ Hazel St., Oneonta, NY 13820; **exhaust fan** by NuTone; **faucet** by Grohe America, Inc.; **financial consideration** by Rodale Press, Inc; **floor finish** by Glitsa American, 327 S. Kenyon St., Seattle, WA 98109; **fluorescent lighting** (UC 15CB) by Power Products Co., Cayuga and Ramona Sts., Philadelphia, PA 19120; **food processor** by Cuisinarts; **ground-fault circuit interrupters** by Square D Co., 1601 Mercer Rd., Lexington, KY 40511; **Health Education computer bulletin board** by Health Education Electronic Forum, P. O. Box 546, Ames, IA 50010; **lacquer and tung oil** by Mohawk Finishing Products, Inc., Amsterdam, NY 12010; **lighting** by DuroTest Corp., North Bergen, NJ 07047; **plastic shelving** by Rohm and Haas, Independence Mall West, Philadelphia, PA 19105; **portable induction cooker** by Sanyo Electric Inc., 200 Riser Rd., Little Ferry, NJ 07643; **pot rack** by Taylor & Ng; **refrigerator/freezer** by Amana; **sinks** by Luwa (stainless steel) and Stanadyne (sink and faucet); **skylight** by Paeco; **stainless steel panels** by Ken St. John, 9 Reynolds La., Woodstock, NY 12498; **Standard 110VAC Performance Pak Actuator** by Saginaw Steering Gear Division, General Motors Corp., Saginaw, MI 48605; **support rails and linear bearing pillow blocks** by Thomson Industries, Inc., Manhasset, NY 11030; **water treatment system** by Amway Corp., 7575 E. Fulton Rd., Ada, MI 49355; **wiring** (Plugmold) by Wiremold Co., W. Hartford, CT 06110; **additional sponsor** is *Journal of Dietetic Software*, P. O. Box 2565, Norman, OK 73070.

"A Kitchen Created by an Aesthetect" (pp. 92-93): **kitchen design** by John Calella, 80 Murray Ave., Kentfield, CA 94904, and Bruce Sexauer, Aesthetect, Sexauer Woodwork & Design, Foot of Spring St., Sausalito, CA 94965; **cabinets and countertops** custom-made by Bruce Sexauer; **commercial range** by Wolf Range Co.; **floor covering** is Italian terra-cotta tile; **lighting fixture** custom-made by Bruce Sexauer; **refrigerator** by Kenmore; **tile work** by Norman of San Francisco Tile Company.

"Opening Up the Galley" (pp. 94-95): **kitchen and architectural design** by Richard R. Heinemeyer, Architect, 180 Cook St., Denver, CO 80206; **cabinets and countertop** custom-made and surfaced with Nevamar India Spice laminate; **cooktop** by Thermador; **dishwasher, oven/microwave unit, and refrigerator** by GE; **floor covering** of 4-by-8-inch quarry tile made by Endicott Clay Products Co.; **sink** (stainless steel double sink with built-in drainboard) by Elkay.

"A Compact Kitchen" (pp. 96-97): **kitchen and architectural design** by Huston Eubank, AIA, CSI, Architect, Eubank and Cantwell, 4 Queen St., Charleston, SC 29401; **general contractor** was Tom Robinson, 105 E. Bay St., Charleston, SC 29405; **cabinets** by Hugh and John Jeffers, JMO Woodworks, 1859 Summerville Ave., Charleston, SC 29405; **countertop** is Formica laminate; **dishwasher** by Modern Maid; **faucets** by American Standard; **food processor** by NuTone; **range** by Magic Chef; **refrigerator** by Sub-Zero; **sink** by Kohler.

"A Kitchen That Lets the Sun Shine In" (pp. 98-99): **kitchen design** by Sears Barrett, AIA, Equinox Design Group, 6000 S. Ulster St., Suite 206, Englewood, CO 80111; **cabinets and countertops** custom-made from Formica laminate by C. & G. Woodworking, 10314 S. Dranfeldt Rd., Parker, CO 80134; **cooktop** by Thermador; **dishwasher** by GE; **faucet** by Hansa, available from Santile International Corporation; **intercom** on wall by phone is by NuTone; **light fixture** by Peerless Electric Co.; **microwave** by Litton; **oven** by GE; **sink** by Alape, available from Santile International Corporation; **tile** on countertops is Italian tile from Designer Tile Gallery, Denver, Co.; **floor** is Mexican tile from Country Tile, Denver, Co.; **trash compactor** by GE.

"A Kitchen of Swirls and Details" (pp. 100-101): **kitchen and architectural design** by Kendrick Bangs Kellogg, Architect, 838 Balboa Court, San Diego, CA 92109; **craftsman and designer** was John Vugrin, Star Rte. 2, Santa Ysabel, CA 92070; **cabinets** custom-built by John Vugrin; **cooktops** (magnetic) by Fasar; **oven** by Thermador; **refrigerator** by Sub-Zero.

"Making the Most of His Lot" (pp. 102-3): **kitchen design** by Richard M. Sibly, AIA, presently of The Martin Organization, 5600 Roswell Rd., Suite 145W, Atlanta, GA 30342; **bar top** is made from oak stair tread and trimmed in poplar; **cabinets** by Geba from West Germany, available through Kitchens from Germany, Ltd.; **cooktop** by Thermador; **countertop** is Duropal laminate from Kitchens from Germany; **dishwasher, oven, and refrigerator** by Kenmore; **floor covering**

is oak; **sink** by Elkay with **faucets** by Delta; **stools** from Storehouse, 2737 Apple Valley Rd., Atlanta, GA 30319.

"A Kitchen for a Family to Grow In" (pp. 104-5): **kitchen design** by Suzanne G. Bates, Buffalo Design Group, R. D. 1, Box 10A, Riegelsville, PA 18077; **renovations** to addition designed by Jeff Iobst, J. A. Iobst & Co., 1560 Graham St., Fountain Hill, PA 18015; **cabinets** by William L. McCarthy, Cabinetmaker, R. D. 1, Box 147, Riegelsville, PA 18077; **countertop** is Corian by Du Pont; **dishwasher** by KitchenAid; **range** by Jenn-Air; **refrigerator** by Frigidaire; **sink and faucets** by Moen; **tile** from Moravian Pottery & Tile Works.

"A Study in Contrasts" (pp. 106-7): **kitchen design** by Craig Bomboy, Bomboy Laminates, 5 Race St., Catasauqua, PA 18032; **bar sink** by Kohler; **cabinets** designed and built by Bomboy Laminates from Formica laminate; **carpentry** by Richard J. Groller, 3303 N. 4th St., Hokendauqua, PA 18052; **cooktop** by Thermador; **countertop** is Formica laminate; **dishwasher** by KitchenAid; **faucets** by Kuri; **kitchen sink** by Blanco; **microwave** by Sharp; **oven** by Thermador; **refrigerator and freezer** by Sub-Zero; **TV** by RCA.

"A Grand Country Kitchen" (pp. 108-9): **kitchen design** by Barbara Bollinger; **beaded floorboards** and other millwork custom-milled by Ritter & Smith Co., 1223 Gordon St., Allentown, PA 18102; **cabinets** custom-built by Brader's Woodcraft Inc., Laurys Station, PA 18059; **cooktop** by Jenn-Air; **countertop and sink** is almond Corian by Du Pont; **dishwasher** by KitchenAid; **faucet** by Harden Industries; **microwave** by Litton; **ovens** by Thermador; **paint for trim** was custom-mixed; **refrigerator** by Amana; **reproduction Windsor chairs** from Frederick Duckloe & Brothers, Inc., P. O. Box 427, Portland, PA 18351; **stenciling** by Karen Prinkey Stenciling, 435 Belfast Rd. Nazareth, PA 18064; **windows** with extra-wide mullions and individual lights custom-made by Marvin Windows.

"A Kitchen by the Sea" (pp. 110-11): **architect** was David J. Shaw, AIA, P.O. Box 337, John's Island, SC 29455; **kitchen design** by Linda Lewis and Claudette Pimm, St. Charles of Charleston, Inc., 1926 Savannah Highway, Charleston, SC 29407; **cabinets** by St. Charles; **cooktop** by Jenn-Air; **countertop** is Formica laminate, with butcher block on the island; **dishwasher** by GE; **disposal** by Thermador; **faucet** by Delta; **floor covering** is Celebrity pattern by Parkett Flooring; **microwave** by Panasonic; **refrigerator** by GE; **sink** by Elkay; **wall covering** by Seacrest Handprints.

"A Respect for Tradition" (pp. 112-13): **kitchen design** by Harry H. Williams, Williams-Builder, 2365 Rt. 33, Robbinsville, NJ 08691; **cabinets** custom-built by Harry H. Williams; **cooktop** by Gaggenau; **countertop** of white Italian tiles; **tile** on the hearth under the woodstove and on the sideboard handmade by Patricia Tanis Sydney; **woodstove** by Vermont Castings, Inc., Prince St., Randolph, VT 05060.

"A Kitchen Personalized for the Long Term" (pp. 114-15): **kitchen design** by Linda and Tom Gettings; **cabinets** custom-made by Richard C. Weinsteiger, R. D. 4, Boyertown, PA 19512; **ceiling** custom-milled by R. C. Weinsteiger of beaded tongue-and-groove mahogany; **ceiling fan** by Casablanca Fans; **countertop** is butcher block; **dishwasher** by GE; **entertainment equipment** by RCA TV; **floor covering** is Bruce hardwood flooring laid in a herringbone pattern with quarry tile in refrigerator room; **built-in furniture** custom-made by R. C. Weinsteiger; **lighting** fixture over island custom-made by R. C. Weinsteiger and hanging lamps over sink assembled by Tom Gettings from separately purchased components; **range** by GE; **refrigerator** by Kenmore; **sink and faucets** by Kohler; **tile** from Sikes Corp. (red tile) and Moravian Pottery & Tile Works (decorative tile).

"A Kitchen with a Sound View"(pp. 116-17): **kitchen design** by Allen D. Elliott, AIA, 4200 Aikins Ave., S.W., Seattle, WA 98116; **cabinets** custom-built by Carlos Sabich, de Carlo Woodworking, 13623 184th Ave. NE, Woodinville, WA 98072; **ceiling** of drywall and clear, tongue-and-groove cedar; **cooktop** by Jenn-Air; **dishwasher** by Hotpoint; **faucets** by Moen; **oven and refrigerator** by GE; **sink** by Kohler.

"A Kitchen with a Garden View" (pp. 118-19): **kitchen design** by Richard Elmore, Richard Elmore Design, Inc., 522 Ramona St., Palo Alto, CA 94301; **cabinets** by Richard Elmore Design, Inc.; **computer** by Apple Computer, Inc., 20525 Mariani Ave., Cupertino, CA 95014; **cooktop** by Jenn-Air; **countertop** is plastic laminate; **dishwasher** by KitchenAid; **faucets** by Delta; **floor covering** is ceramic tile; **oven and refrigerator** by GE; **sink** by Elkay.

"Rescuing a Poor Design" (pp. 120-21): **kitchen design** by Robert L. Wieland, CKD, Kitchens by Wieland Inc., 4210 Tilghman St., Allentown, PA 18104, and Iris Konia, Iris Konia Interiors, William Penn Plaza, Easton, PA 18042; **cabinets** by Style Craft Kitchens, Inc., of Formica 920 Almond and 903 Terra Cotta (island); **cooktop** by Jenn-Air; **countertop inlay** next to sink is tempered glass by Phoenix Glass Products, Inc., 444 Hempstead Tpk.,

West Hempstead, NY 11552; duck decoys are from collection of owner; **dishwasher** by KitchenAid; **flooring** is oak finished with polyurethane; **microwave** by Litton; **conventional ovens** by GE; **refrigerator** by Sub-Zero; **sink** by Elkay, **faucets** by Moen; **tiles** on countertops are Portuguese tiles by Elon.

"David's Kitchen" (pp. 122-23): **kitchen design** by Linda Ziegenfuss; **ceiling** material is tongue-and-groove cedar with V-groove edges and stained with cherry; **countertop** is Formica; **dishwasher** by White-Westinghouse; **faucets** by Moen; **floor covering** of bricks by Passeri Marble and Tile Inc., 241 N. Cedar Crest Blvd., Allentown, PA 18104; **lighting** is track lights over dining counter and recessed lights over range and counters by Lighting Fixture and Supply Co., Inc., P.O. Box 1228, Allentown, PA 18105; **microwave** by Minutemaster; **range** by Jenn-Air; **refrigerator** (side by side) by Hotpoint; **sink** by Kohler.

"A Kitchen with Contemporary Curves" (pp. 124-25): **kitchen design and construction** by Ed Kaschel, Cabinet Gallery, Inc., 4878 W. Seneca Tpk., Syracuse, NY 13215; kitchen design by Pamela M. Speer, Pamela M. Speer Interior Design, 7495 Northfield La., Manlius, NY 13104; **built-in toaster** by Modern Maid; **cabinets** are Millbrook Euro 2000; **compactor, cooktop, dishwasher, and oven/microwave** by Whirlpool; **Char-Glo** grill by Thermador; **countertop** is Formica edged with brushed chrome; **faucets** by Delta; **hot-water dispenser** by Elkay; **refrigerator** by Sub-Zero; **sink** by Elkay; **stereo** by Yamaha; **tile** is by Rico; **TV** by Zenith; **wall covering** by Morton Jonap, Ltd., 12 Midland Ave., Hicksville, NY 11801.

INDEX

Boldface page numbers indicate entry in table. Lowered page numbers indicate illustrations.

153